Story, Song & Dance

Jean Gilbert

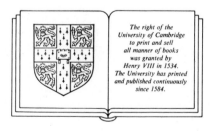

The right of the
University of Cambridge
to print and sell
all manner of books
was granted by
Henry VIII in 1534.
The University has printed
and published continuously
since 1584.

Cambridge University Press

Cambridge

New York   Port Chester   Melbourne   Sydney

Published by the Press Syndicate of the University of Cambridge
The Pitt Building, Trumpington Street, Cambridge CB2 1RP
40 West 20th Street, New York, NY 10011, USA
10 Stamford Road, Oakleigh, Melbourne 3166, Australia

First published 1990

Printed by Bell and Bain Ltd., Glasgow

Illustrated by Pauline Woloshin

ISBN 0 521 33967 7

ME

Acknowledgements

Publisher's acknowledgements

Many of the items in this book are in copyright. For details, please refer first to the page on which the item appears. If application is made in writing, the Permissions Controller of Cambridge University Press will endeavour to forward correspondence regarding permission to private individuals. The following items are in the copyright of publishers and other institutions. They may be contacted direct.

Every effort has been made to reach copyright holders. The publishers would be glad to hear from anyone whose rights they have unknowingly infringed.

"Lucy Ladybird" by Betty Root, an adapted version of the story of the same name originally published by Good Reading, 1974; "Something inside me" by Kenneth Simpson, reproduced from *77 Rounds and Canons* by permission of Novello and Company Limited; 1st verse of "Caravans' by Irene Thompson, from *Poems for the Very Young*, reproduced by permission of Unwin Hyman; "The fun of the fair", arranged by Sidney Northcote, from *The Clarendon Singing Course*², © 1955 Oxford University Press; "Stone Soup", adapted from Mavis

Micklethwaite's *A Wall for the Cuckoo*, Macdonald 1974; "Breakfast" by Adrian Rumble, from *A Shooting Star* (Poetry 2), published by Basil Blackwell Ltd; "Mustard" by Ogden Nash, from *Custard and Company*, Kestrel Books 1979, poems © 1979 by the Estate of Ogden Nash; "Spaghetti" by Shel Silverstein, from *Where the Sidewalk Ends*, published by Jonathan Cape Ltd; "Salt, mustard, vinegar, pepper", arranged by Anne Mendoza and Joan Rimmer, reproduced by permission of William Elkin Music Services on behalf of J. Curwen & Sons Ltd; "Professor Noah's Spaceship", adapted by Jean Gilbert from the story of the same name by Brian Wildsmith, Oxford University Press 1980; "Africa" by pupils of The Butts County Primary School, Hampshire, arranged by Christopher Norton, from *Sounds Natural – A Wildlife Song Book*, © 1983 World Wildlife Fund, sole agents Boosey & Hawkes Music Publishers Ltd, reprinted by permission; "Leave Them a Flower" by Wally Whyton, © 1969 Durham Music Ltd, 19/20 Poland Street, London W1V 3DD, international copyright secured, all rights reserved, used by permission; "Margaret and the Mermaid" by Grace Hallworth, from *Mouth Open Story Jump Out*, Methuen Children's Books Ltd 1986; "Sea Creatures" by Maria Gonzalez, from *Feelings*, The New Voices 1977.

SONG BOOKS and MUSICAL ACTIVITY BOOKS published by Cambridge University Press

Seasonal Songs by Dot Paxton
A collection of easy-to-learn songs for each season of the year with ideas for 'spin-off' work
ISBN 0 521 33668 6

Story, song and dance
For the young, a collection of ideas for improvised drama with music, compiled by Jean Gilbert
Book   ISBN 0 521 33967 7
Cassette   ISBN 0 521 32758 X

Music through topics by Veronica Clark
An activity resource book and cassette for teachers of 4- to 8-year-olds
Book   ISBN 0 521 34842 0
Cassette   ISBN 0 521 35630 X

Titles in the CAMBRIDGE YOUNG MUSICALS series

The Bells of Lyonesse
ISBN 0 521 33590 6

Seaspell
Piano/Conductor edition ISBN 0 521 33588 4
Performers' edition ISBN 0 521 33589 2

Duffy and the devil
Piano/Conductor edition ISBN 0 521 33592 2
Performers' edition ISBN 0 521 33593 0

African Madonna
ISBN 0 521 37880 X

🔈 denotes items on the cassette (ISBN 0 521 32758 X) which accompanies this book. The cassette can be ordered through a bookshop or, in case of difficulty, direct from the Educational Sales Department, Cambridge University Press.

It is hoped that the cassette will provide suitable guidelines for teachers, especially those who do not read music, and that both teachers and children will enjoy listening to the songs.

They include a selection of the percussion suggestions from the teaching notes; however, teachers are reminded that in the classroom the children should be encouraged to invent their own accompaniments wherever possible and they may therefore prefer to introduce any listening with the children after the songs have been taught. The music for the country dances is intended as a resource for the teacher both in the teaching and performance of the dances.

Contents

Introduction

This book presents ten units, each containing material and practical suggestions based on an integrated approach to music, movement and drama.

Each unit includes:
- a story
- a dance (one or more) or dramatized movement suggestions
- related musical activities such as simple sound accompaniments, instrumental improvisations, sound pictures, word rhythm games, making up tunes
- a song (one or more)

The theme of each unit is associated with a popular classroom topic and it is hoped that this link will add to versatility and usefulness in the classroom.

The units themselves have been developed with the wide range of age and ability of young children in the primary school in mind. Thus some of the stories and activities will be found to be more suitable for the 5- and 6-year-olds while others will be enjoyed by older age groups. They all provide opportunities for teachers to encourage the creative and imaginative abilities of their children whether they are developed as a basis for classroom activities or as a small 'item' presented within the school or to parents.

Each story has a different potential which is reflected in the suggested activities, but cross-references may provide teachers with further ideas for a particular story or topic.

Links can be made with other areas of the curriculum such as art and language. It is hoped that teachers will explore a wide range of activities to encourage each child to contribute and to draw upon the varied creative talents that young children possess.

Guitar chords have been suggested where suitable. They have been chosen to support the melody when accompanied by the guitar alone, and do not necessarily reflect the harmony implied in the piano accompaniments.

A teacher's guide to the topics covered by each unit is supplied on pages 6–7, with ideas for further 'spin-off' work. Obviously these are interrelated and ideas cross from one area to another.

A teacher's guide

	Age range	Themes	Music
Lucy Ladybird	5–7 years	Minibeasts Colours and patterns in nature Insects: structure, movement	Sound pictures Word rhythm games Making up tunes Song with percussion
The Green Galumpetty Monster		Monsters/giants Food Colour	Sound picture Sound poem Two songs with percussion suitable for movement
Moon Lake	6–9 years	Large animals, e.g. elephants Small animals, e.g. rabbits Jungles Water India	Sound pictures Bengali songs
Ma Liang and his Magic Brush		Magic China Movement of people Storm at sea	Percussion accompaniment for play Song with percussion to perform separately or with play
The Emperor's Oblong Pancake		Change Shape and size, especially round, oblong	Rounds Songs that go together Improvisation leading to composition based on rondo form Song with percussion to perform separately or with play
The Fairy at the Fair		Fairs: modern and historical Fairies and other legendary folk Fairground movement	Sound picture Making up tunes for fair cries Ensemble work Musical games Two fairground songs with percussion suitable for movement
Stone Soup		Cooking Taste Introduction to the subject of unemployment	Word rhythm games Musical soup – ensemble playing Songs that go together – three-part song with percussion and recorder
Professor Noah's Spaceship	7–10 years	Pollution Conservation (wildlife at risk) Animals, birds, butterflies, plants Forests	Sound picture Sound poem Making up tunes Two songs: 1 folkstyle 2 with percussion
Eggo the Robot		Computers/robots Mass production	Machine sounds Sound pictures Making up tunes Sound sequence leading to dramatization of the story Song with percussion to perform separately or with drama/movement
Margaret and the Mermaid		The sea: its moods Marine life Seafood Fishing	Sound pictures Sound and movement poem Song to perform separately or to support movement or drama

Drama/Movement	Art/Craft work	Language	Maths and other extensions
Movement leading to mini-ballet – percussion accompaniment	Colour/pattern Frieze linked with reading	Word rhythms related to music Storytelling sequence	Number sets
Monster/scarecrow movement	Colour: green Puppets Collage	Alliteration Animal 'voices' Words describing movement of monsters, giants, large animals Puppet play	
Movement leading to dramatization of story – percussion suggestions	Size and shape relating to animals Collage frieze	Words describing large animals and their movements Words describing small animals and their movements Descriptions of water: sight, sound Introduction to written scripts, e.g. Bengali	Contrasts: size, shape, movement
Mime and movement in preparation for play	Experiments with different implements and materials Story friezes Scenery for play	Storytelling Story writing	
Movement to do with shape Choreography Country dancing – circle and lengthways Outline for a play with song and dance	Bubbles Frieze related to shape Painting	Words to describe shape, size, direction Making up poems	Shape, size Tessellation
Movement related to fairground amusements Movement and mime – at the fair	Working models: fairground machines Frieze	Fair cries Story writing	Money Number guessing games History of fairs
Cooking movement sequences Miming/dramatizing the story sequence	Food textures	Sounds and movements related to cooking Word rhythms Recipes Making up verses	Weighing and measuring (food)
Animal movements leading to forest sequence Robot movement Building the spaceship	Collage	Animals: sounds, movements Sounds in the forest Story writing	
Mechanical and robotic movement Group work Choreography – robot ballet	Modelmaking of robots	Instructions Mechanical movements	Repetition
Movement to do with the sea, marine life, life in a coral reef, by the shore, life in the depths	Frieze	Sounds of the sea Story extension	Life in the Caribbean

General notes on the activities

This section outlines a general approach to the suggested activities included in the units. Teachers who may require more detailed information are referred to the book list at the end of this section.

Using instruments

Young children need a great deal of experience in handling instruments, listening to the different sounds they can produce and learning to accompany and play together before they are ready to contribute to specific activities in a way that they can understand and enjoy. This involves making the instruments available, allowing time for the children to experiment with them and talking about the sounds they have made.

Teachers may be reluctant to organize percussion groups where every child has an instrument. However, this is one way of involving all the children at the same time and provides a general experience on which to build. The smaller the group, the better. Larger groups require a tighter discipline, perhaps an inner circle to play, an outer one to listen. Circumstances vary.

Sit the children on a carpet if possible, in a circle around the instruments. Begin as soon as they have all chosen an instrument. Ask them to make a beautiful sound and to stop when you signal. They can play quietly, loudly, quickly, slowly, watching all the time for your signal. *Change instruments frequently*.

They can play sounds for a giant stomping, a mouse scurrying, clouds floating by, water dripping. They can accompany you walking round, stopping when you stop. You could skip, hop, run. How would they change their rhythm and speed?

Dance a nylon scarf. Make it float, wave up and down, wriggle, drop to the ground. The sounds change each time.

Listen to the sounds from metal, wood, plastic material. Which instruments produce long/short sounds? Gradually encourage the children to choose the most suitable instrument for different effects and types of movement.

With pitched percussion it is most unlikely that there will be an instrument for every child. One way is to introduce the instruments, one at a time, and to explore with the children different ways of playing them: a glissando or gentle glide up and down, a trill or 'shiver', moving the beaters over a group of two or three notes, a jumping or step-by-step pattern.

Discuss the sounds produced by different beaters; always have a variety available. Leave an instrument in the music corner when suitable for the children to handle on their own. Make a work card to guide their playing.

Sound pictures

In a way, the children have been producing very simple sound pictures during their exploratory work in the percussion groups already described. It is easy to build on this experience.

Tell them that a sound picture is like a painting in sound. Show them a picture: a windy day or an underground cave, for example. What sounds would they hear? What sounds would help to create an atmosphere?

Keep the children in circle formation with instruments in the middle. Choose a sound picture, then hear as many sounds as you can from the children. Talk about them before deciding which sounds to have and who will play them. Conduct the children with agreed signals for starting and stopping. Later on the children themselves can decide how to combine their sounds into a short composition. Ask them to think more carefully about how they will play and to listen to the sounds of other players.

Older children will enjoy a greater challenge and they will need to think about patterns and shapes (form) to guide their playing. Here are some approaches to consider:

Form	Sound pattern
A persistent background of one or two sounds; other sounds come and go, singly, in pairs or in groups.	A _____ B _____ C D E
Two different sections (binary form):	Part A – Part B
Two sections with the first one repeated (ternary form)	A B A
Cumulative **a** A gradual build-up, then tail off	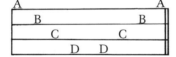
b A gradual build-up to a climax	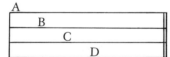
Rondo form: This has a recurring section.	A B A C A D A

The use of various instruments is suggested throughout the book. These instruments are illustrated here:

clappers

bells

sticks

guiro

kazoo

cymbals

recorder

drum

swanee whistle

xylophone

maracas/shakers

gong

tambourine

triangle

glockenspiel

wood block

tambour

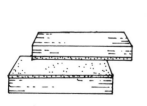

finger cymbals

sand(paper) block

NOTE These instruments are not drawn to accurate relative scale.

Simple composition

Making up tunes

This activity will be more successful if the children have had plenty of experience with both pitched and non-pitched percussion as suggested in the previous section.

Chime bars are easiest to use with young children. If a xylophone or glockenspiel is used, remove all the notes except the ones needed for playing. A larger (alto) xylophone is preferable as it supports the pitch range of the children's voices.

1 Begin by introducing simple 'tune play' with just two notes, E and G. This could take the form of an echo game using the rhythm of the children's names:

Play and sing *Don-na*. Children echo *Don-na*.
          G E   G E

Let the children play their own name tunes for the class to echo back. While each child has a turn, show the others how to tap out the rhythm of their names; this will involve them all and provide rhythmic practice at the same time.

Continue with these two notes G and E, extending the length of the phrase. Try snippets of conversation, "Good morning, everyone", or a statement, "Johnny's wearing blue shoes".

Allow the children time to experiment with the chime bars in the music corner. Give them a simple work card to start them off. Felt beaters give an acceptably quiet sound!

2 When the children are ready, introduce new notes A and D in that order. Further activities can include:

a Question and answer:

Hallo Marlene, how are you?
G E G E   G A G

Very well, thank you
G A G E   E   G

b Using longer phrases based on sequences like the days of the week, or shopping lists, or linked with words related to ongoing topics or centres of interest:

Worm caterpillar spider   ant
A   G G G G   E D   E

c Working on short rhymes like 'Rain, rain, go away'.

Always encourage the children to sing their tunes afterwards. This helps them to remember them.

3 The final notes to add are bottom C and top C. These two notes complete the pentatonic or five-note scale on C. The advantage of this set of notes for the early stages of tune making is that it is within the singing range of young voices and that tunes can begin and end on any note. Of course, a pentatonic scale can start on any note, for example on G: G A B D E G.

The children will soon be ready to make up longer tunes. Choose any short children's rhyme, or perhaps the children themselves could make up a simple couplet or short verse and set it to music.

Ensemble playing

The next step to making up a tune is creating a simple accompaniment. The following suggestions illustrate various ways of doing this, starting with very simple ideas and progressing to those that involve several children or the whole class.

1 The tune is accompanied throughout by simple percussion:

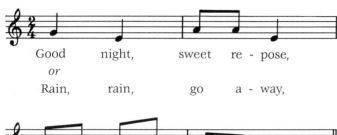

Good night, sweet re - pose,

or

Rain, rain, go a - way,

Half the bed and all the clothes.
Come a - gain a - noth - er day.

Here are three different ways of adding an accompaniment:

a Playing on every word:

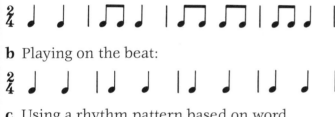

b Playing on the beat:

c Using a rhythm pattern based on word rhythms taken from the tune:

(Sweet re- pose)

2 The tune could be repeated two or three times to lengthen it and make it a more interesting piece. The first time a shaker could accompany, the second time a tambourine and finally a tambour or all three. This arrangement would suggest a gradual increase in dynamics, starting quietly and ending fairly loudly.

To involve all the children, double up on the instrumental parts and ask the non-players to sing. Here is a simple arrangement:

a Singers whisper the rhyme in rhythm.
b The tune is played.
c The tune is sung and played.
d The percussion instruments accompany the tune as suggested above to provide an instrumental interlude.
e Everyone sings and plays to finish.

3 If a number of pitched instruments are available, the children can be introduced to the idea of group improvisation.

Each child has an instrument with all the notes removed except C D E G A C, or with just the notes that have already been introduced. Establish a rhythm based on a simple rhyme like the ones suggested above and let the children experiment with a tune. Play the rhyme over and over again. Other children can help by whispering the words in rhythm or by playing quiet percussion instruments to support the rhythm.

This was an introduction. By now the players will have discovered several tunes that they like. Let them each play their tunes to one another. If they can remember one of them for the next part, all well and good; otherwise they can continue to improvise.

One player begins and plays or improvises a tune twice through. The next player does the same while the first player continues. Each player joins in until they are all playing together. It is important to maintain a strict rhythm throughout and for the children to use control and restraint in their playing. Interest can be maintained by varying the dynamics, getting quieter or louder. Ask the children how they would like to end their ensemble – stopping one by one, or all together, or in groups.

4 This is a more structured approach to ensemble playing using three or more pitched instruments.

First of all establish a basic tune which all the children can learn to play. It is essential that they can play it easily before adding the other parts:

a A drone. This consists of one, sometimes two notes played together, and repeated throughout. It is usually played on a low-pitched instrument.

b An ostinato is a short, repeated melodic and/or rhythmic pattern. Several different ostinati could accompany the main tune.

Here is an example of an arrangement for a simple ensemble group:

TUNE

Je - re - mi -ah blow the fire, Puff, puff, puff!

First you blow it gent - ly, Then you blow it rough.

DRONE

OSTINATO 1

(Je - re -mi - ah blow the fire. . .)

OSTINATO 2

(Puff, puff, puff!)

There are many different ways in which these parts could be combined. Here is one way:

The drone plays for four bars and continues.
Ostinato 2 plays for two bars and continues.
Ostinato 1 plays for two bars and continues.
The tune joins in and plays through three times, the last time being quiet. The other instruments quieten.
Ostinato 1 stops after two bars.
Ostinato 2 stops after two bars.
The drone plays for four bars and ends the piece.

Further parts could be devised using non-pitched instruments, but it would depend on the overall 'sound'.

Useful books

Children Dancing: Practical Approach to Dance in the Primary School Rosamund Shreeves (Ward Lock Educational, 1979).

Experiments in Sound Gertrud Meyer-Denkmann (Universal Edition, 1977).

Exploring Sound June Tillman (Stainer & Bell, 1976).

Musical Starting Points Jean Gilbert (Ward Lock Educational, 1981).

Sound Waves: Practical Ideas for Children's Music Making Leonora Davies (Bell and Hyman, 1985).

Lucy Ladybird

Lucy Ladybird lived with her family in a large garden. She was a very beautiful red ladybird with seven large black spots.

One day when she was resting by the pond admiring her reflection in the water, she caught sight of those seven large black spots. She was horrified.

"My beautiful red back is quite spoilt," she said to herself. "Whatever can I do to get rid of those spots?"

She flew up to speak to her wise friend, the owl.

"Friend Owl," she said. "I hate my spots. How can I get rid of them?"

"Your spots!" replied the owl, "I like your spots." And he sat there blinking his big, round eyes at Lucy.

So she flew off to visit Queen Wasp. "Perhaps she can tell me what to do," thought Lucy.

Queen Wasp looked at Lucy carefully. "Your spots?" she said, "Why, they are nearly as pretty as my stripes, z z z z z . . ." And she stretched out her long black and yellow body.

Lucy saw the spider watching her from the middle of his web, and decided to ask him. She crawled carefully nearer to speak to him.

"I hate my spots," she told the spider. "How can I get rid of them?"

The spider did not move. "Come closer," he whispered, "and I will rub them off." Lucy was frightened by the sticky web and quickly flew away.

Then she noticed the caterpillar painting a picture down by the pond. She had an idea and hurried across.

"I hate my spots. Please paint them away," she pleaded.

Caterpillar mixed some colour and soon all the spots had disappeared.

Lucy flew straight down on to a water lily to look at herself in the water. Yes, the spots had all gone. Her beautiful red back glistened in the sunlight. She would show all her friends.

She waved to the dragonfly as he came past, but he just flew away without waving back. Then she saw the bumble bee and the butterfly and waved to them, but they flew by without even noticing her. It seemed that none of Lucy's friends recognized her.

Lucy was sad. She wondered why her friends did not want to come and see her now that her horrible black spots were gone. She looked at her reflection again but this time she slipped and fell into the pond. She splashed around and by the time she had struggled out of the water all the paint had washed away. Lucy looked bright and sparkling in the sun. She stayed on the water lily drying herself in the warm sunshine.

Then, one by one, all her friends hurried down to see her.

"Wherever have you been?" they asked her. "We have been looking for you everywhere."

"I have been here all the time," Lucy laughed. She forgot about her spots now that she had her friends to talk to.

Adapted by Jean Gilbert from an original story by Betty Root

General notes

'Lucy Ladybird' is a lovely story for younger children, particularly suitable for summer reading and one that can inspire a variety of classroom activities. Here are some suggestions:

1   Encourage the children to retell the story. Can they remember the sequence of visits Lucy made to her friends? How did each respond? What colour did the caterpillar use to paint away the spots? Why did Lucy's friends not recognize her without her spots? What was the most important thing to Lucy?

2   Let each child write and draw one episode from the story. Mount these in a class story book.

3   Make a classroom frieze of the story. Link with reading by including the snippets of conversation that occurred between Lucy and her friends.

4   Encourage the children to study the natural colour and patterning of each creature in the story. Provide templates or let the children draw freehand. The pictures can be coloured in, cut out and decorated and assembled in group or individual collages of the story.

5   Make a set of ladybirds with different numbers of spots. These can be used to sort into number sets or used in a game of Snap.

Explain to the children that the coloured parts of the ladybird with the spots are the front wings or wing cases. These are used as a hard cover to protect their bodies. Ladybirds have flimsy back wings for flying which are folded up under the coloured wing cases.

Movement

Introduce all the characters, building on the children's observation where possible. The movement can be done with or without accompaniment.

Ladybird

Soprano glockenspiel   At rest, knees bent, torso leaning forward with arms 'folded' behind to portray oval-shaped back. Arms can open as back wings in flight. Wings beat so quickly they almost seem to be still. Lands on a water lily to dry. Has a brief sunbathe.

Owl

Alto metallophone or xylophone   Sits on the branch of a tree, shoulders hunched to indicate feathered back and neck. Head turns from side to side, eyes blinking slowly. In flight, arms stretched to portray large wingspan. Wings beat slowly with big movements. On landing, this big bird takes a little time to settle, folding back its wings purposefully, then watches out for the next meal.

Queen Wasp and Bumble Bee

Kazoo   In flight, fussy, buzzy movements, searching for nectar and pollen. Arm movements light and taut to indicate fragile wings. They fold back when feeding.

Spider

Drum or tambour, scratched/tapped   A crouched position for the spider waiting in his web. In movement, the spider can be very slow or extremely fast; movements can be unpredictable. Children can go on all fours or walk bent over with arms as front legs.

Caterpillar

Sand block or guiro   Long, thin body. Children imitate the caterpillar's 'humping' movement as it travels along.

Dragonfly

Alto glockenspiel   Long, thin body, arms stretched wide as thin, delicate wings. The flight is very fast with little darting movements, hovering over a water lily, then skimming just above the water before resting on a flower. Short stay before taking off again.

Butterfly

Bells   Very graceful movements. Arms as wings can flutter. Flight is erratic. Butterfly rests on a flower. Children can kneel with arms held high and as far back as possible.

Follow up the general movement in more detail.

1   Choose two characters with distinctive movements and percussion. The children change characters as the accompaniment changes and freeze in the silences.

2   Repeat with the children working with partners. This time they only portray one character, so they freeze when the other one is moving. Sometimes play the two accompaniments together to encourage a duet in movement. Involve the chidren in the accompaniments.

3   Continue in the same way with three, perhaps four characters if you think the children are ready – they have to be good listeners! Keep to the same instrument for each character.

4   Partners can now join up to work in fours, two playing and two moving.

5   The foregoing suggestions could easily lead to the children devising their own mini-ballet

Lucy Ladybird

with a small group of musicians and dancers. This could be quite simple, involving only a few of the characters in improvised movement, or more elaborate and possibly based on the theme of 'Lucy Ladybird'.

6 Sing the song for 'Lucy Ladybird', on pages 20–21. This could be used to support a simple dramatized version of the story.

Musical activities

Sound pictures

The use of percussion should be linked with the suggestions for movement accompaniments in the previous section so that there is no confusion about which percussion instrument is linked with each character.

Let the children choose which characters they would like to include in their sound picture. Keep it simple at first by limiting the number to three or four. As the children become confident, build up to add variety and to provide a greater challenge.

Sit the children in a working circle with instruments in the middle. Divide them into groups of their choice and allow time for each group to work out a suitable sound pattern to represent each character. This can include stopping and starting, changes in dynamics (loud/quiet) and variations of speed. The children can also use their voices for Queen Wasp, Bumble Bee and Owl.

Work out with the children a general pattern for their sound picture: a sequence of entries, when groups play together, how to finish and so on. It is important that they listen to one another. Conduct the children with agreed signals or choose a child conductor according to the previous experience of the children.

Another approach to a sound picture is to base the sequences on a simple narrative, either the Lucy Ladybird story itself or something the children have suggested.

Story	Sound picture
Ladybird flies down to Caterpillar	Glockenspiel – gentle glissando with added shaker
Caterpillar greets Ladybird	Guiro or sand block
They 'talk'	Instruments play together
Butterfly and Dragonfly come and go	Sounds from bells and alto glockenspiel
Owl warns of approaching spider	Voices or xylophone Tambour/drum plays, getting louder
Ladybird and Caterpillar escape	Guiro/sand block and glockenspiel/shakers get quieter
Spider crawls away	Sounds from tambour/drum get slower and finally stop

These sound pictures could also provide accompaniments to the children's movement.

Word rhythm games

Choose the names of four characters with distinctive word rhythm patterns, for example:

		Claps
Ladybird	♫ ♩	* * *
Spider	♩ ♩	* *
Caterpillar	♫ ♫	* * * *
Owl	♩	* *hold*

Prepare picture or name cards for each character. For children who have already been introduced to rhythm notation, the cards could include the music notes on the back.

Establish a steady beat, then ask the children to:
say and clap each word;
whisper and clap each word;
think and clap each word.

Do this several times until the children have learnt the rhythm associated with each word. They are now ready to play some of the following games.

1 Divide the class into two or more groups. Give each child a turn at clapping one of the cards. Which group scores the highest correct responses?

2 Keep to the same groups. Put out three cards. Clap the rhythms in any order several times with the children joining in. A child from the first group volunteers to put the cards in the order in which they have been clapped. Each group has several turns. Which group scores the highest? Increase the difficulty of the game by putting out all four cards.

3 Hold up a card for one child to clap. If she gets it right, it is her turn to choose another card for her neighbour to clap. The game proceeds until all the children have had a turn. It may be necessary to have a 'referee' (who could be the teacher or another child) to decide on the correctness of the responses.

4 Choose a child to play a drum in the middle of a circle. Establish a steady beat. The drum plays two beats, rests for two beats, continuously.

♩ ♩ rest rest ♩ ♩ rest rest ♩ ♩ etc.

While the drum plays, hold up different cards. The children respond immediately by clapping the name rhythms in the rests.

5 The same game can be played with individual children clapping the rhythms in

sequence round the circle. Let the children work on some of these ideas in the music corner, in pairs. The rhythms could be played on a quiet instrument; for example, one child plays a rhythm, the other one picks up the correct card.

Making up tunes

Refer to the Introduction. Encourage the children to make up simple tunes based on these word rhythms using notes from the pentatonic scale according to their previous experience, for example:

Using notes D E G A

La-dy-bird,   ca-ter-pil-lar,   spi-der,   owl.

Similarly, rhythms from simple rhymes could be used, for example:

Ladybird, Ladybird,
Fly away home.
Your house is on fire
And your children all gone.

Incey Wincey spider
Climbing up the spout;
Down came the rain
And washed the spider out;

Out came the sunshine
And dried up all the rain;
Incey Wincey spider
Climbing up again.

Music for listening and moving

Flight of the Bumble Bee Rimsky Korsakov
'The Insect Parade' from *Child Education: Music and Movement* cassette (Scholastic Publications Ltd, Westfield Road, Southam, Leamington Spa, Warks CV33 OJH)

Lucy Ladybird's song

Words and music by Jan Holdstock

Note The guitar chords fit the tune but don't go with the piano accompaniment.

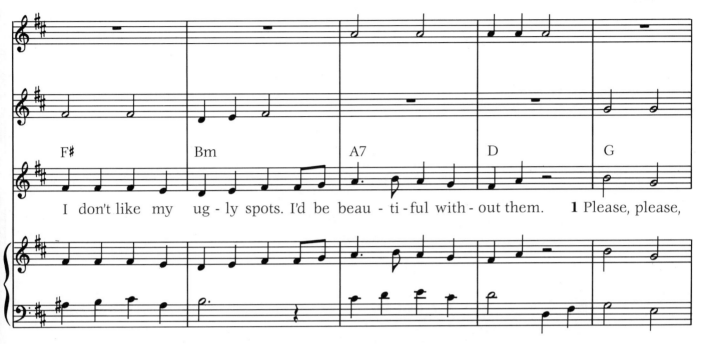

I don't like my ug-ly spots. I'd be beau-ti-ful with-out them. **1** Please, please,

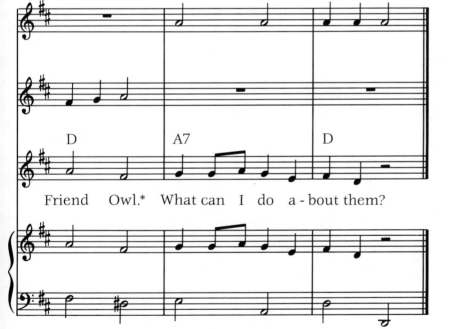

Friend Owl.* What can I do a-bout them?

Optional verses

1 2 3 4 5 6 7 spots of ugly black
1 2 3 4 5 6 7 up and down my back.
Now you've painted out my spots,
I am beautiful without them.
Caterpillar
Knew what to do about them!

1 2 3 4 5 6 7 spots of pretty black
1 2 3 4 5 6 7 up and down my back.
Now I love my pretty spots,
I was nobody without them.
Hello everyone!
I'm very glad about them!

(*spoken*) Your spots! I like your spots.

* Verse 2 Please, please, Queen Wasp . . .
  (*spoken*) Your spots! Why, they are nearly as pretty as my stripes.

* Verse 3 Please, please, Spi-der . . .
  (*spoken*) Come closer and I will rub them off.

* Verse 4 Please, please, Ca-ter-pil-lar . . .

The Green Galumpetty Monster

The Green Galumpetty Monster was lost, and it was all his own fault. He had been grazing up on Monster Mountain, and his mother had told him to *stay right there*, where she could see him.

"Humph, why?" said the Green Galumpetty Monster, all sulky.

"Because you'll get lost", said his mother. "Come and eat this Good Green Grass, there's a good boy."

But the Green Galumpetty Monster wasn't good. Outside he said "Yes Mother", but inside he said "NO."

You see, he didn't want Good Green Grass. He didn't want Munchy Moss or Licky Leaves either. What he wanted was the Tiny Tasty Turnip Tops he had heard about – the ones which grew in a field somewhere at the bottom of the mountain.

When his mother's back was turned, he did a sneak and a slink, then another sneak, all the while going further away down the mountain.

Wasn't he shocking?

When at last he reached the bottom, he found himself clumping along a winding country lane. He wasn't at all sure of the way to the turnip field, so it was lucky he met a Scarecrow and was able to make enquiries.

Where's the turnip field?" he bellowed rudely. He was bigger than the Scarecrow and felt like showing off.

"Say please", said the Scarecrow.

"Humph, why?" said the Green Galumpetty Monster.

"Why not?" said the Scarecrow.

"Because I'm a Green Galumpetty Monster, and we don't do things like that."

It was shocking the fibs he told when his mother couldn't hear him.

"No? What *do* you do then?" asked the Scarecrow, interested.

"Oh, well, we bellow a lot, and howl and growl and go HUMPH! Like this." And he howled and growled and went HUMPH.

"Very nice", said the Scarecrow, impressed. "Anything else?"

"Yes", said the Green Galumpetty Monster. "We steal Tiny Tasty Turnip Tops. And I'm hungry. So where's the turnip field?"

Now the Scarecrow thought it was nice that Green Galumpetty Monsters howled and growled and went HUMPH. But it didn't think it was at all nice that they stole Tiny Tasty Turnip Tops. So it said, very fast:

"Left – right – right – then left – then under – then over – then right again, right?"

Which was completely wrong.

But it didn't much matter, because the Green Galumpetty Monster didn't know right and left anyway. Living on a mountain, he only knew up and down.

He clumped and galumphed this way and that, sometimes going right and sometimes left and occasionally under and over, until he was completely lost. By now, his feet hurt and it was starting to rain. Also, it was getting dark. Worse still, he was horribly hungry, but when he looked around for something green to eat, there wasn't anything'!

The country lane had become a big wide road lined with tall houses which made him dizzy. The fields had vanished, and even the trees were strange. They were stiff and straight, and grew lights at the top instead of branches.

Then, out of the night came a roaring howl – and two huge yellow eyes were glaring at him. The Green Galumpetty Monster leaped out of the way just in time, and the Yellow-eyed Beast went rushing past, screeching and smelling of smoke.

It was all too much. The Green Galumpetty Monster slumped down and buried his face in his pink paws.

PINK paws?

I'm afraid so. You see, Green Galumpetty Monsters start to fade if they don't eat Regular Green Meals. Oh dear, what a disaster.

A big green tear rolled down his cheek, then a pink one.

"What's up, sonny?" asked a kindly voice. A man with a black pointed head was bending over him.

"I'm lost", snuffled the Green Galumpetty Monster, forgetting to howl or growl or even HUMPH. "I'm a Green Galumpetty Monster, except I'm pink now because I haven't eaten any greens lately. And my mother's going to be *ever* so cross!"

"I see. And where do you live?" asked the man, who was of course a policeman.

"Monster Mountain."

"My, you *are* a long way from home. You've come all the way to town! You'll just have to come back to the station. Too late to go home tonight."

So the Pink Galumpetty Monster went humbly to the station, where the policeman dried him off and gave him a bowl of sprouts to try and turn him green again.

They didn't work. *Regular* Green Meals are what count.

The next day, the policeman hired a big red bus and drove him back to Monster Mountain, where his mother was waiting for him.

She made him eat Good Green Grass for days and days until, finally, he turned green again.

He didn't mind.

He liked grass.

He *loved* it.

It was his favourite.

Kaye Umansky

General notes

Suggested activities for extending the story with younger children:

1 Encourage the children to retell the story. Individual children could describe each episode in the correct sequence. What kind of monster was this one? Why was he green? What were the strange trees that grew stiff and straight with lights at the top? What was the Yellow-eyed Beast that went rushing past?

2 What other 'colour' monsters can the children describe, for example:

Red Roaring Monster
Blue Bouncing Monster
White Whispering Monster

Can they make up their own monster story?

3 The monster ate a diet of green food which kept him in good shape as a green monster. What was his diet? What kind of foods do the children like? Do they know in what ways particular foods help to build their bodies? This aspect of the story would link well with a food project.

The Green Galumpetty Monster

4 Art and craft could include drawings, paintings, collages of the story, of the monster, the scarecrow, the policeman and the big wide road at night. A collage of green foods could lead into a colour project.

5 Puppets of the monster and its mother, the scarecrow and the policeman could be used by the children to make a puppet play of the story.

Movement

Let all the children have fun interpreting the movement of the main characters.

Monster

The words of the song will help the movement. Bodies are big and a little bit lumpy, faces are grim and grumpy. The children can thump, stump, and bump around – but not too heavily, for this is a baby monster! Sometimes the children can be scary and scowly and move with a bonk and a clonk. Let them move around, then freeze into monster statues.

Scarecrow

Practise thin, spiky shapes and jerky movements. Again let the children move around, then freeze into scarecrow statues.

Policeman

Children walk tall with slow measured steps. They can practise controlling traffic and patrolling their 'beat'.

Duet

Working with a partner, the children can choose which two characters they would like to be. They move, then freeze, alternately. The changes can be made by an agreed signal, or different percussion instruments can accompany the movement. It is easier if the children choose the same two characters to begin with. Later on they can work in fours, two moving and two playing.

A link with language can be made by asking the children to think of descriptive words that can be reflected in their movement. This will also suggest the type of percussion that could accompany some of the movement. Here are some suggestions to consider:

Monster
Tambour or bass drum and padded beater
Alto or bass xylophone – random notes
Slow bass notes on the piano; occasionally a cluster of notes pressed down firmly

Scarecrow
Sticks; guiro; shaker

Policeman
Tambour or tambourine; wood block

Excerpts from the following recorded music could also be used:

Monster
'Elephant' or 'Lion', from *Carnival of the Animals* Saint-Saëns

Scarecrow
'Machines and Robots' from *Child Education: Music and Movement* cassette, side 2 (Scholastic Publications Ltd, Westfield Road, Southam, Leamington Spa, Warks CV33 OJH)

Policeman
Florentine March Fučik (or any march tune)

Duet
Listen, Move and Dance, No. 4, side 2, band 3: 'Discussion' (EMI CLP 3531)

Musical activities

The children can imagine that they have gone to explore the land of the Green Galumpetty Monsters. They have built themselves a hide and observe several families of the monsters as they approach and pass the children who remain unseen. They have, however, taken a tape recorder and camera with them to make records of their visit. The following ideas for a sound picture could be recorded and played to illustrate the children's paintings and other art and craft work. It could also be used as an introduction to a puppet play of the story.

Sound picture

Roars	A gong or deep-toned tambour, or some metal, like the bottom part of a budgie cage shaken carefully, will give a monster-like sound
General movement	Tambours, drums, played with a padded beater
	Alto and/or bass xylophone
	Tambourines and shakers to increase the sound as the monsters stomp past
Trampling of undergrowth	Clappers, sticks, sand blocks
Growls, grunts, hisses	A small group of children can work out a pattern of sounds with their voices

Work out with the children a pattern of sound for the general movement. This can get louder as the monsters approach and quieter as they go away. Bring in the growls and atmospheric sounds at agreed times and with agreed signals.

Sound poem

Ask the children to talk about the sounds these monsters might make. Compile a class poem and add sound effects.

> I'm a Green Galumpetty Monster,
> Thump, thump, thump.   (*Tambour*)
> I'm a Green Galumpetty Monster,
> Stump, stump, stump.   (*Tambourine*)
> My eyes go click,   (*Wood block*)
> And my mouth goes clack.
> My green scales rustle on my back. (*Shaker*)
> Listen as I mooch about,   (*All together*)
> I might go 'Humph!' if you don't shout!

Poetry collections

The following collections include some amusing verses about animal monsters:

Milliganimals Spike Milligan (Puffin Books, 1971)

Seeing and Doing ed. Rosalind Farrimond (Thames Television, 1985)

Silly Verse for Kids Spike Milligan (Puffin Books, 1970)

The Green Galumpetty Monster

Green Galumpetty Monsters

Words and music by Kaye Umansky

Rhythmically

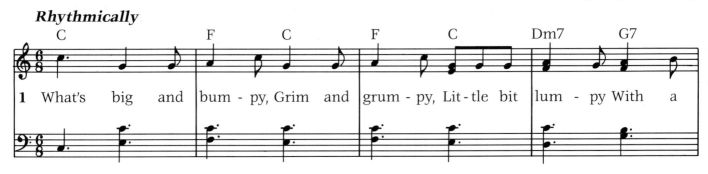

1 What's big and bum-py, Grim and grum-py, Lit-tle bit lum-py With a

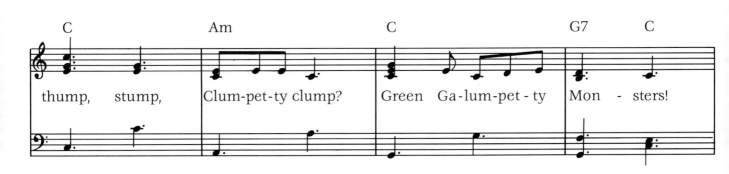

thump, stump, Clum-pet-ty clump? Green Ga-lum-pet-ty Mon - sters!

CHORUS

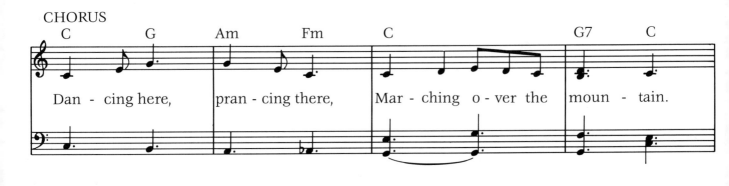

Dan - cing here, pran - cing there, Mar - ching o - ver the moun - tain.

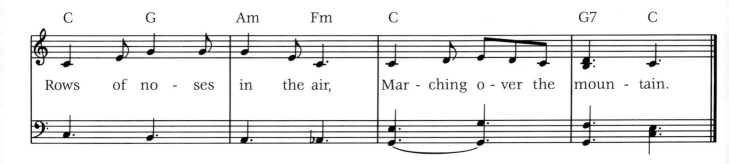

Rows of no - ses in the air, Mar - ching o - ver the moun - tain.

2 What's scary scowly,
Hairy howly,
Little bit growly?
With a bonk, clonk,
Honketty honk,
Green Galumpetty Monsters!
CHORUS   Dancing here, prancing there, etc.

Suggested percussion

Try these patterns with the song:

DRUM

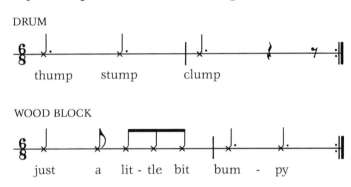

WOOD BLOCK

MARACAS

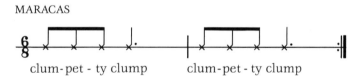

The Green Galumpetty Monster

Land of the monsters

Loud and slow

Words and music by Jean Gilbert

1 Stomp, stomp, stomp, We're in the land of the mon - sters,

Stomp, stomp, stomp, See them lum - ber a - long, _____

Snar - ling, grow - ling, his - sing, roar - ing,

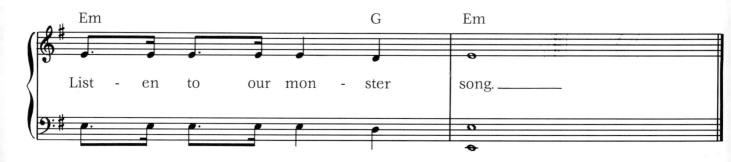

List - en to our mon - ster song. _____

2   Creep, creep, creep,   (*Quiet and slow*)
    This monster goes very slowly,
    Creep, creep, creep,
    See him steal along,
    Looking, listening, stopping, watching,
    Listen to our monster song.

3   Run, run, run,   (*Quiet and fast*)
    This monster goes very quickly,
    Run, run, run,
    See him race along,
    Quick as lightning, quiet as grey cloud,
    Listen to our monster song.

4   Roar, roar, roar,   (*Loud and fast*)
    This monster goes very quickly,
    Roar, roar, roar,
    See him thunder along,
    Lashing, crashing, twisting, turning,
    Listen to our monster song.

Suggested percussion

Choose a different percussion instrument to accompany each verse. A simple rhythm based on the words 'Stomp, stomp, stomp'

is effective, or encourage the children to use their own ideas.

ALTO XYLOPHONE

Movement

The words of this song will suggest different types of monsters and different ways of moving. Use the same percussion chosen by the children for the verses.

Moon Lake

Once upon a time in a far-off jungle there was a large lake of clear water surrounded by tall trees and beautiful shrubs. A herd of elephants lived nearby and every day they came to drink and play in the lake and to feed on the green leaves growing around it. They were ruled by a mighty elephant king who looked after them with love and kindness. With plenty to eat and drink and no worries, the elephants spent their days peacefully.

One summer it became very hot and no rain fell for a long time. All the streams ran dry and the elephants' lake became smaller and smaller until it was clear that all the water would soon be gone. The elephants realized that if they could not find more water soon many of them would die. So they gathered around their king and asked him to help them.

The king knew that there was no time to waste. He selected the fastest elephants in the herd and commanded them to search in every direction and not to return until they had found water.

The elephants searched for water day and night without rest until one of them found a beautiful clear lake.

Following their king the herd reached the lake as quickly as they could and rushed into the water, drinking, playing and splashing around all day long until they were completely exhausted, and then they fell asleep.

Little did they know that they were being watched by hundreds of rabbits who lived around the lake. The rabbits were terrified because in their hurry to get to the water the huge elephants had trampled many of them underfoot. They knew that if they did not act quickly, soon none of them would be left alive.

That night the rabbit king called an urgent meeting to find ways to get rid of the mighty elephants. Many suggestions were considered but rejected as they would not have worked. Nobody could think of any real solution. The rabbit king was utterly dismayed – he knew that the huge elephants would soon destroy them all.

Just then the moon rose in the sky and its light was mirrored in the pool. A clever rabbit who was quietly sitting at the back stood up and announced that he had thought of a plan to solve the problem. If it succeeded the elephants would never return to the lake again.

Next day the rabbit saw the elephants going towards the lake. He jumped onto a big rock and, facing the elephant king, addressed him in a loud voice:

"Oh mighty elephant king, please listen to me."

The elephant king paused and looked in the direction from where the voice came.

"I am the messenger from the moon", said the rabbit. "He is the master of the whole universe and this lake belongs to him. He is very angry with you for polluting its water with your big feet and for killing the rabbits who are under his special protection. He is going to teach you a lesson by withholding his light from your herd unless you come to him and ask his forgiveness." On hearing this the elephant king trembled with fear.

At nightfall the elephants led by the rabbit reached the lake. The reflection of the full moon was shimmering in the clear water. The rabbit asked the elephants to step into the water and bow to the moon. The elephants bent their heads and dipped their trunks in the water. It made the water ripple, which shook the moon as if he was angry. The more the elephants bowed the more the moon shook.

"We cannot live here because the moon is very angry with us", said the elephant king. "He will punish us severely if we stay any longer."

Quickly he collected his herd and started back into the jungle. As they were fleeing from the lake, large drops of rain began to fall. At last the rain had arrived and the elephants went happily back to their own home.

Indian folk tale retold by Elizabeth Sharma

General notes

This story comes from a collection of tales known as the Panchatantra. These tales form part of the ancient, almost timeless folklore of India and were first written in Sanskrit about 200 BC. Before that they had been related by storytellers for about 3,000 years.

The tales were originally told to three little Indian princes by their teacher, Vishnu Sharma. These young princes were lazy boys who, to the despair of their father, the king, displayed no interest in their studies. Eventually, an old sage was found who succeeded in finding a way of educating the princes. Day after day, Vishnu Sharma told them stories of great wisdom and common sense in which most of the characters are animals who think, talk and behave like human beings. It is these stories that have come to be known as the Panchatantra Tales.

The activities outlined here are more suitable for younger children although the story itself will appeal to children of all ages.

1 Ask the children about the story. Why did the elephants leave their own lake? Why was water so important to them? What prompted the rabbit to think of a way to get the elephants to go away? What other method might have worked? Encourage the children to retell the story.

2 Let each child write and draw an episode from the story. Mount in a class story book.

3 Prepare a jungle background for a frieze with a lake and moon in the centre. Let each child contribute a painting or crafted cutout of an elephant, a rabbit and a tree, designed as an exercise in size. With the help of the children, assemble the collage to interpret the story.

4 Discuss with the children what part water plays in their lives. Can they remember any hot summers that have been very dry and any local water restrictions that may have resulted? What do campers do about water?

5 Tell the children how the Panchatantra Tales came to be written. The word *Panchatantra* means 'Five Books'. Show the children on a large globe where India is and compare it in size with the UK. Make a collection of suitable picture and information books, for example *India* in Macdonald's Looking at Lands series and *India: The Land and Its People* in Macdonald's Countries series (see 'Useful books', page 38). Enlist the help of Indian children and their parents. Perhaps some of the parents might be able to talk to the children about India and bring in some pictures and photographs or some objects like clothing or jewellery.

6 Make a book of drawings and pictures about elephants in India. Tame elephants are used in a number of ways, such as to help with heavy work like forestry clearance, to provide transport and to take part in ceremonial occasions. Make a large model of an elephant. Refer to the Indian story 'The Six Blind Men and the Elephant' (see 'Useful books' on page 38).

Moon Lake

Hathi · Elephant song

Words by Roma Gupta   Music by Pratibha Chaudhuri

Slow

Kay cho-le-che oi cho-le-che, Gah du-lee-yeh sur ghu-ree-yeh,

Hat-hi__ cho-le - che O bhai hat-hi__ cho-le - che.

Bod-do bha-reeh sho-reer tar-e-eh, Ti-re-er mo-ton da-a-ter gah-tan,

Bee-rat__ bee-rat pay-e-er bha-ree Sho-hor__ to-lee - che, O bhai

hat-hi__ cho-le - che. Kay cho-le-che oi cho-le-che,

Gah du-lee-yeh su-r ghu-ree-yeh, Hat-hi__ cho-le - che O bhai

hat-hi__ cho-le - che, O bhai hat-hi__ cho-le - che.

Accompany with a deep-sounding drum or tambour:

36

হাতী

Hathi

ঐ কে চলেছে ঐ চলেছে,

Kay choleche oi choleche,

গা দুলিয়ে শুঁড় ঘুরিয়ে,

Gah duleeyeh sur ghureeyeh,

হাতী চলেছে ও ভাই হাতী চলেছে।

Hathi choleche o bhai hathi choleche.

বড্ডো ভারী শরীর তারই,

Boddo bhareeh shoreer tareeh,

তীরের মতন দাঁতের গঠন,

Tireer moton daater gahtan,

বিরাট বিরাট পায়ের ভারে

Beerat beerat payeer bharee

শহর টলেছে,

Shohor toleeche,

ও ভাই হাতী চলেছে।

O bhai hathi choleche.

Look, there is an elephant.
  The elephant is walking.
His body is swinging from side to side
  And his trunk is curled up.

His body is very heavy
  And his tusks are like spears
And his legs are so heavy
  That the towns and cities are trembling.

Bengali script, transliteration and translation by Roma Gupta

Moon Lake

Khorgosh · Rabbit song

Words by Roma Gupta   Music by Pratibha Chaudhuri

Fairly quick

Nōw   tu - mee raaj - hash _ nōw _ tu - mee boo - no-mosh,

Cho - to khaa - to sho - ree - reyr   sa - da rong   kho - r - gosh.

Tu -   mee   sa - da rong   kho - r - gosh.

Chhu - tey jaoo   dru - too ta - ley   ba - ree ghor   chhou - ta - ley,

Ma - te - er to - la - tey jaoo _   kha - kha - nōw _ bhai _ pe - le.

Nōw   tu - mee raaj - hash _ nōw _ tu - mee boo - no - mosh,

3 times

Cho - to khaa - to sho - ree - reyr   sa - da rong   kho - r - gosh.

Accompany with a tambourine:

খরগোস
Khorgosh

নও তুমি রাজহাস নও তুমি বুনোমোষ,
Nōw tumee raajhash nōw tumee boonomosh,

ছোট খাটো শরীরের সাদা রং খরগোস।
Choto khaato shoreereyr sada rong Khorgosh.

তুমি সাদা রং খরগোস।
Tumee sada rong Khorgosh.

ছুটে যাও দ্রুত তালে বাড়ী ঘর চৌতালে,
Chhutey jaoo drutoo taley baree ghor chhoutaley,

মাটীর তলাতে যাও কখনও ভয় পেলে।
Mateer tolatey jaoo khakhanōw bhai pele.

You are not a swan,
    You are not a wild bull,
You are a rabbit with a small body
    And white colour.
    You run very fast,
You move round everywhere –
    In and out of the house,
But when you are afraid
    You hide in a hole.

Bengali script, transliteration and translation by Roma Gupta

 *Moon Lake*

Movement

The elephant and the rabbit provide perfect examples of contrasts in size, shape and movement. Much of the movement will relate to these contrasting features. The following notes include suggestions for instrumental accompaniments, but much of the introductory movement could be done unaccompanied.

The elephants

Encourage the children to think of descriptive words like 'big', 'huge, 'strong', 'leathery', and movement words like 'lumbering', 'plodding', 'rushing', 'thundering' (refer again to the story of 'The Six Blind Men and the Elephant').

Children move like elephants, then freeze into a strong shape. Accompany with a deep-sounding tambour or drum. They move again and next time make strong shapes with a partner. Suggest different ways and speeds of moving, also different groupings for when the children stop and 'hold' their shapes.

They imagine a deep lake, shallow at the edges. As elephants, some fully grown, some quite small, they wade into the water to drink and play. They improvise movement sequences in groups.

The rabbits

Children think of descriptive words like 'small', 'furry', 'timid', and movement words like 'hopping', 'running', 'loping', 'burrowing'.

They move like rabbits, freezing into small shapes. Vary the movements each time, running, hopping, loping, then introduce sequences of movement. Accompany with a tambourine.

Children freely improvise on their own, moving, looking for food, eating, twitching noses and ears. They work with a partner or in groups.

Elephants and rabbits

Alternate elephant and rabbit movements working with the group as a whole. Children can now choose, responding to their own instrument and freezing while the others move. Change over. Encourage children to take over the accompaniments.

Children work with partners improvising a duet between a rabbit and an elephant.

Divide the children into rabbits and elephants to interpret the incident at the lake. Choose two kings.

Story line	Suggested accompaniment
Rabbits move around the lake.	Tambourine
They run away as elephants rush into the water to drink and play.	Drum/tambour Xylophone (*ripples*)
Elephants rest.	
Rabbits hold a meeting	Tambourine
Moon rises over lake.	Cymbal
Rabbits disperse except for one.	Tambourine
Rabbit meets elephant king and leads herd to lake.	Tambourine and drum
Elephants bow to moon.	
Water ripples.	Xylophone
Elephants troop away.	Tambour/drum
Rabbits return to eat and play.	Tambourine

An approach through movement based on these suggestions could be made to a dramatization of the complete story.

Musical activities

The following suggestions for small groups are outlined as a guide to the children's music-making or for more detailed accompaniments for the movement as required.

Music for elephants

Ask the children to choose instruments to convey the size of the elephants and their great lumbering movements. These can include both pitched and non-pitched instruments – tambour, drum, wood block, guiro, xylophone, metallophone – depending on what is available at the time. Let them all play together to get the feel of a slow beat. Discourage the tendency to play loudly to convey size at this stage!

Improvise with the children a phrase or rhyme using some of the descriptive words from the movements, for example:

Elephant, elephant, big and strong,
*　　　　*　　　　*　　　　*
Great thick legs that plod along.
*　　　　*　　　　*　　　　*

Accompany with a slow beat as indicated.

Next try slightly quicker beats for elephants running, for example:

Elephant, elephant, big and strong,
*　*　　*　*　　*　*　　*
Great thick legs that lumber along.
*　　*　　*　*　　*　　*　　*

Sound picture: Elephants in the jungle

Group 1: Elephants	Tambour/drum/ alto/bass xylophone
Group 2: The jungle	
Undergrowth being crunched	Paper/plastic egg carton
Branches swaying	Tambourine
Branches cracking	Wood block
Insects	Comb and tissue paper
Birds	Recorders

Children in group 1 work out a sequence for the elephants. Children from group 2 can then add the jungle sounds in a pre-arranged order.

Moon Lake

Music for rabbits

Ask the children to choose instruments to represent rabbits, thinking back to the descriptive words used in their movement. Some children may have pet rabbits; there may even be a rabbit in school so there may be an opportunity to study its domestic habits (refer to an illustrated edition of *Watership Down*).

The tambourine has been suggested in the 'Movement' notes because it can accompany hopping and jumping movements as well as the twitching, fussy movements when the rabbit is still or eating, but the children will think of a variety of instruments.

Concentrate first on the characteristic hop which becomes a fast lope when the rabbit is moving at speed. Word rhythms can help the children to begin with. Improvise a suitable rhyme with the children, for example:

Rab - bit stop, rab - bit hop,
*   *   *   *   *   *
Up and down, hop and stop.
*   *   *   *   *   *

Practise playing together, hopping and stopping, then try some slightly faster hopping movements.

Now divide the children into two groups. The first group work out a sequence to represent the rabbits moving around. The second group add sounds for when the rabbits stop to eat.

Water music

Ask the children to describe pools or lakes they have seen. They may think of ripples, splashes, shadows, reflections. What might we see in and around the water? Reeds, insects, birds, fish. . . Are any movements rhythmic at all? Some are, some are not. This music will be mainly impressionistic.

When the children have chosen their instruments and practised their sounds, discuss with them how they can arrange their playing to make an interesting sound picture. Here is just one suggestion:

Water ripples	**Glissandi** on xylophone/ glockenspiel/metallophone
Occasional splashes	Quiet bells
Reeds rustling	Shakers
Shoals of small fish	Finger cymbals
Bigger fish	Two or three deep-sounding chime bars – felt beaters
Reflections shimmering	Several chime bars played with ruler or strip of card wobbled over sound hole
Birds	Recorder tops – hand wobbling over end
Insects	Sand block
Frogs	Guiro
Moon rising	Big cymbal – padded beater

Suggested arrangement

Sounds of the water and reeds play throughout in a prepared sequence. The other sounds come and go on their own or in groups. At the end the moon rises, then the sounds of the water gradually fade.

Music for listening and moving

Carnival of the Animals Saint-Saëns ('The Elephant', 'Kangaroos' and 'Aquarium')

Short excerpts of Indian classical music can be used to introduce the story or a dramatized version of it. Suitable records or cassettes may be available through the school collection or from the local education authority, the local library or from parents. However, here are some current titles:

Bismillah Khan – shehnai (wind instrument) (EASD 1373)

Hari Prasad Chaurasia – chaurasia (flute)
  (Eternity ECSD 2988)
Ravi Shankar – sitar (strings) (EASD 1502,
  also EASD 1421)

Useful books

Activities and Projects: India in Color Claude
  Soleillant (New York: Sterling, 1979)
Family in India ed. Peter Otto Jacobsen and
  Preben Sejer Kristensen (Wayland, 1984)
India Patricia Bahree (Macdonald Educational,
  Looking at Lands series, 1985)
India Zaidee Lindsay (A. & C. Black, 1977)
India Is My Country Cliff and Bernice Moon
  (Wayland, 1983)
India: The Land and Its People Natasha
  Talyarkhan (Macdonald Educational,
  Countries series, 1975)
Moon Lake, retold by Elizabeth Sharma (Tiger
  Books, Panchatantra series, 1985)
The Blind Men and the Elephant Paul
  Galdone (World's Work Children's Book, 1963)

Ma Liang and his Magic Brush

Once upon a time there was a boy named Ma Liang whose father and mother had died when he was a child. He lived in a village in China where he earned a living by gathering firewood and cutting weeds.

Now the one thing that Ma Liang longed to do was to paint, but he was so poor that he could not even afford to buy a brush. So he used twigs from firewood to draw birds on the sand. He dipped his finger into the water when cutting weeds and traced fish on the rocks and found charred wood to sketch on the walls of his cave. He made up his mind to learn and practised hard every day. His pictures were so good they almost came to life!

One night when he was fast asleep after a busy day, an old man appeared holding a golden brush. "This is a magic brush," he said. "Use it carefully!" Before Ma Liang had time to thank him the old man vanished. Ma Liang woke with a start. Had it been a dream? But there by the side of his bed was a golden brush.

He couldn't wait to try out his new brush. First he painted a bird. He watched in amazement as the bird came to life. It flapped its wings and soared up into the sky singing merrily. Then he painted a fish which plunged into the river outside and darted away. Ma Liang took his magic brush everywhere. He painted every day for the poor folk in the village: a plough, a hoe, an oil lamp or a bucket for the families that needed them.

The news of Ma Liang's magic brush began to spread. One day a rich landlord heard about it. The greedy man captured the poor boy and tried to force him to paint gold ingots. Ma Liang despised the landlord. "You don't need any more gold," he said. "It's the poor people who need my help." The angry landlord ordered Ma Liang to be locked up without food.

Ma Liang joined other prisoners who sat shivering and hungry. Then he remembered his magic brush. First he painted a stove for warmth and then some cakes. The grateful prisoners warmed themselves and ate until they were satisfied. Then Ma Liang painted a ladder to lean against the wall. All the prisoners followed Ma Liang up the ladder and over the wall, escaping into the darkness.

Very soon the sound of the landlord and his men could be heard. Ma Liang quickly painted a fine horse and galloped away down the highway. He rode on until he came to a small village. He decided it was safe to stay there, but it was a long way from his own home. He could find no work so he kept himself busy and happy by painting for poor people.

Ma Liang became known for his kindness. One day he painted a big ox to help an old man who was struggling to plough a field with bare hands. Another time he painted a water wheel to help a farmer whose crops were almost dried up.

Once again, news of the magic brush spread until it reached the ears of the emperor, a cruel man who hated people. Officers were sent to summon Ma Liang to court.

Ma Liang knew about the emperor's cruelty and was not going to serve him. When ordered to paint a dragon he painted a toad instead which leaped and flapped around the emperor. The emperor was furious. He seized the magic brush and threw Ma Liang into prison.

Then he tried using the magic brush himself. First he painted a gold mountain, then another and another, but they all turned into a pile of rocks. Then he painted a long golden bar but this turned into a python which rushed at him with its huge mouth open. He was terrified. Luckily his officers quickly caught the terrible monster.

By now the emperor realized that the magic brush would not work for him. He released Ma Liang and promised him riches and a princess in marriage if he would paint for him. Ma Liang, who had already formed a plan, pretended to agree.

The emperor ordered Ma Liang to paint the sea. Sure enough, a clear, boundless sea appeared before them. Then he ordered fish and a boat to sail out to sea to watch the fish. Ma Liang painted a huge sailing boat which the emperor boarded, followed by the empress, princes, princesses and many ministers. He drew the wind with a few strokes and the boat moved off. But the wind was not strong enough for the emperor. Ma Liang's magic brush brought a strong wind. The sea grew rough. A few more strokes and the sea roared, big waves rolled and the vessel began to keel over.

"Enough, enough wind!" shouted the emperor, but Ma Liang paid no attention. A hurricane blew up, the sky darkened and angry waves reared higher and higher. At last the boat capsized and sank with the emperor and all on board to the bottom of the sea.

The story of the emperor spread far and wide. As for Ma Liang, some say that he went back to his native village. Others say that he roamed the earth painting for the poor wherever he went.

Adapted by Jean Gilbert from a Chinese folk tale

General notes

The story of Ma Liang will inspire many classroom activities that can support the working out of the suggested play and add to its success and enjoyment. Here are some suggestions with older children in mind:

1 Encourage the children to retell the story. Organize a story circle. One child begins, then asks a friend to continue. Different children continue until the story is told.

2 Make a classroom frieze of the various episodes. Let the children look at picture books and pictures of Chinese art to get an idea of clothing and the type of countryside in which the story might be set.

Current periodicals like *China Pictorial*, *China Reconstructs*, *Shanghai Pictorial* and *Women of China* are good sources, available from local specialist bookshops or from the Guanghwa Company, 7–9 Newport Place, London WC2H 7JR.

Useful books are:

Chinese Childhood Marguerite Fawdry (Pollock's Toy Theatres, 1977)

The Love of China Anthony Lawrence (Crescent Books, 1979)

Pictures by Chinese Children (Peking: Foreign Languages Press, 1976), available from the Guanghwa Company

3 Let each child choose a part of the story to write and draw. Mount in a group story book.

4 What would the children paint if they had a magic brush, and why? What would they paint if they wanted to help a neighbour, a friend or someone in need? They could make a *Magic Brush Book* and talk about how life could be made happier for everyone.

5 What adventures might the children have if they possessed a magic brush? Ask them to write and illustrate their stories.

Ma Liang and his Magic Brush

6 Ma Liang made drawings with sticks, twigs and charred wood. Let the children experiment with different materials. Perhaps there are some Chinese children in the class who can write in Chinese with a brush.

An outline for a play is given on pages 50–51. Suggestions for movement and music are given in the following sections.

Movement

Introduce all the characters in general movement before casting for the play. Discuss them with the children so that each character is portrayed through the movement. This is best done unaccompanied at first.

Ma Liang

Wanders in the countryside, gathers firewood, weeds, observes nature, draws pictures on the ground, on rocks and on the walls of his cave.

Villagers

Some will be old, moving wearily, some young, moving more freely. Gathering firewood, chopping wood, drawing water from a well, cleaning, sweeping, digging.

Old man

Walks slowly, slightly bent back, kind face, looks around for Ma Liang, slowly puts brush down.

Prisoners

Cold, hungry, sad. Children could mime their reactions to Ma Liang, their amazement at the appearance of the stove and the cakes. They warm themselves and eat with relish.

Landlord

Fat, greedy, stern, comes to look over crops and buildings.

Emperor

Haughty, cruel, walks regally, gives orders.

Bird

Light movements, arms opening as wings in flight.

Fish

Smooth movements, slight wriggle as fish dives, then swift, darting movements as it swims free.

Toad

Arms curved wide, knees bent and broad stance. Ugly hopping, flopping movements as it approaches the emperor.

Python

Thin body, vicious, curling movements, then a swift glide with hands open at chin as python rushes at the emperor.

Encourage the children to imagine how these four creatures would emerge from a painting, come alive and begin to move. In the case of the toad and python, let the children work in pairs, one as the emperor who can react with disgust at the toad and with horror at the python.

What picture does Ma Liang paint?

The children will enjoy miming their own interpretations of Ma Liang's pictures. One child does the painting; a partner mimes, bringing the picture to life. Whoever guesses correctly what the picture is can choose a partner to present another sequence.

Musical activities

Gradually introduce instrumental accompaniments to the movement where applicable, using the same instruments that will be used in the play. At this stage a group of children can be chosen to form an instrumental group.

The final episode, that of the sea and storm, will need more careful planning. There should be a gradual crescendo as the storm develops and a climax when the boat capsizes. Encourage the children to work out a plan among themselves, but here are some suggestions:

Story	Suggested accompaniment
Ma Liang begins painting	Triangle
Little waves	Shakers
Deeper water	*add* Alto xylophone – glides up and (mostly) down with occasional random notes
Wind	*add* Voices
Angry waves	*add* Deep drum and an occasional shake on the tambourine
	A gradual crescendo
The boat capsizes	Drum
	Instruments quieten and stop
The boat sinks	Cymbal roll, gradually quietening
	Silence

Music for interludes

This can be played by recorders and percussion based on the song (see pages 51–53) or can be improvised by the children using the group of notes on which the song is based:

 D E F G A C' D'.

This grouping is called the *Shang mode*.

Alternatively, pre-recorded excerpts of Chinese classical music could be played, for example:

Chinese Classical Music (NWLP 2007) or *Chinese Classical Masterpieces* (Lyrichord 7182)

If there are no suitable school records, try to borrow from the local education authority or from the record collection of the local library.

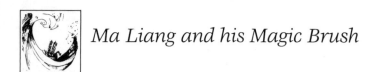

Dramatizing the story

The following suggestions outline ideas for a dramatic extension of the story. They could be used by one or two classes depending on numbers.

Scenery

Two painted backgrounds mounted on screens:

1 Countryside   **2** Prison background

Characters

Ma Liang
Old man with magic golden brush
Villagers – farmers, workers, peasants
Prisoners
Bird
Fish
Rich landlord and his men
Emperor and followers – empress, princes, princesses, ministers
Toad
Python
Narrator
Group of musicians and singers

Narrator introduces the play.
Opening song sung by all. Select verses.

Scene 1 Background 1	Suggested percussion
Ma Liang enters. Works and draws with twigs.	Quiet bells/finger cymbal
He yawns, lies down and falls asleep.	
Old man enters. Puts golden brush down.	Cymbal or gong
Ma Liang wakes up to find the brush.	Finger cymbal
He paints a bird.	Triangle
Bird flies off.	Bells/glockenspiel
He paints a fish.	Triangle
Fish wriggles, plunges into the river outside and swims away.	Xylophone
Paints an oil lamp for villager.	Triangle
Paints a bucket for villager.	Triangle
Enter rich landlord with his men. Ma Liang refuses to paint, is seized by the men and marched away.	Drum

Scene 2 Background 2	
Interlude music as required	
Enter Ma Liang and prisoners. They talk.	
Ma Liang remembers his magic brush and paints a stove and cakes.	Triangle
Real ones appear. The prisoners warm themselves and eat.	
Ma Liang paints a ladder.	Triangle
They all escape.	

Scene 3 Background 1	
Interlude music as required	
Narrator gives an account of Ma Liang's ride and arrival in a distant part of the country.	Quiet drums and coconuts to indicate flight
Enter Ma Liang exploring a new village. He paints an ox for a farmer.	Triangle
He paints a water wheel for another farmer.	Triangle
News of the magic brush spreads.	
Enter two officers who capture Ma Liang.	Drum
Emperor enters. He orders Ma Liang to paint a dragon. A toad appears instead.	Tambourine
Emperor storms away, having seized the brush.	Drum
Ma Liang is taken away and emperor returns with the brush.	

He paints a gold mountain but finds rocks.

Then he paints a golden bar but finds a python. He is terrified until the officers catch it.

Emperor sends for Ma Liang and promises him everything to secure his services.

Ma Liang pretends to agree and begins to paint the sea.

(Blue/green strips of light material are held at each end and lightly shaken.)

Tambourine

Drums, guiro, maracas
(see song, verse 6)

See suggestions for storm music, page 49

Ma Liang paints a royal boat. Emperor and followers embark *(off-stage)*.

Ma Liang begins to paint wind. Voice from emperor: "Enough wind!"

Painting continues until boat sinks.

Enter peasants who rejoice with Ma Liang and invite him back to their village.

Repeat of song, everyone joining in appropriate verses.

Ma Liang's song

Words and music by Gaik See Chew

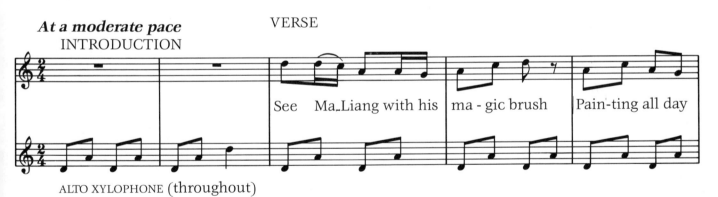

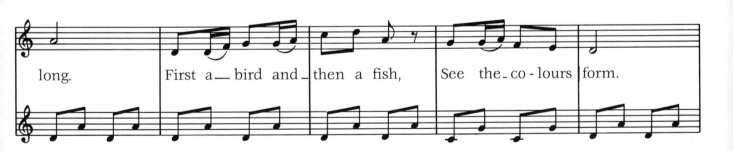

Ma Liang and his Magic Brush

CHORUS

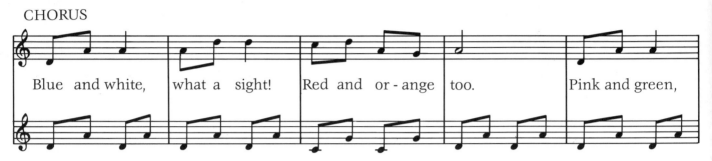

Blue and white, | what a sight! | Red and or-ange too. | Pink and green,

Last verse   *Fine*

what a scene! | See it's like a dream.

1 See Ma Liang with his magic brush
Painting all day long,
First a bird and then a fish,
See the colours form.

CHORUS
Blue and white, what a sight!
Red and orange too.
Pink and green, what a scene!
See it's like a dream.

2 Then he paints to help the poor
Painting all day long,
Ploughs and hoes and buckets too,
See the colours form.

CHORUS   Blue and white, etc.

Suggested percussion

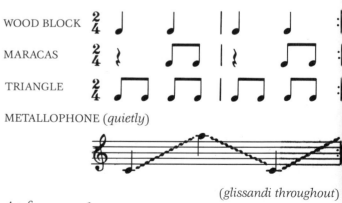

WOOD BLOCK

MARACAS

TRIANGLE

METALLOPHONE (*quietly*)

(*glissandi throughout*)

As for verse 1

3 Now a stove and then some cakes
Painting all day long,
Ladders to lean against the wall,
See the colours form.

CHORUS Blue and white, etc.

4 One day he painted a great big ox,
Painting all day long,
Then he painted a water wheel,
See the colours form.

CHORUS Blue and white, etc.

5 A cruel man the emperor was
And he stole the brush,
Wanted a dragon, *got a toad*! (*spoken loudly*)
See the colours form.

CHORUS Blue and white, etc.

6 Recorders and tuned percussion play while singers hiss and a snake dance is performed.

CHORUS Blue and white, etc.

7 Last he paints a sailing boat,
Painting all day long,
Emperor, princes all afloat,
See the colours form.

CHORUS Blue and white, etc.

As for verse 1

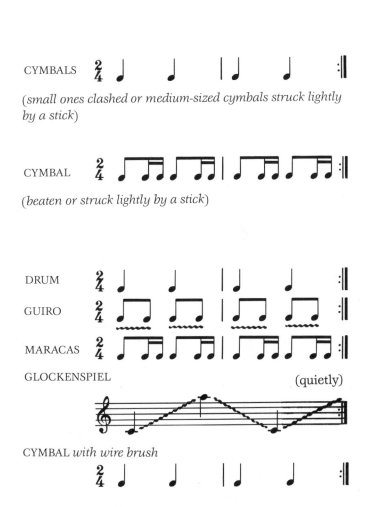

CYMBALS

(*small ones clashed or medium-sized cymbals struck lightly by a stick*)

CYMBAL

(*beaten or struck lightly by a stick*)

DRUM

GUIRO

MARACAS

GLOCKENSPIEL   (quietly)

CYMBAL *with wire brush*

The song should be sung at a moderate pace which should be in keeping with the style of Chinese music.

Melody line This has been specially composed within the range of the descant recorder to provide an accompaniment for the singers.

Tuned percussion A sparse accompaniment on tuned percussion sounds more authentic than the piano. The alto xylophone has been suggested, but any other suitably pitched tuned instrument can be used.

Python episode Here is an opportunity for a long snake to be made. This could be carried on poles or could simply be a long piece of cloth with holes cut in the top for the children to pop their heads through. Otherwise the python could be danced by one of the children using suggestions given in the movement section.

The Emperor's Oblong Pancake

Long, long ago in the East there was an Emperor who loved pancakes. He used to eat six of them for breakfast every day of the year. Great, big yellow ones they were with a bit of brown on top, always done to a turn and round as round can be.

One fine morning in spring the Emperor came down to breakfast feeling very merry because it was his birthday.

"Happy Birthday, your Excellency," said the first footman, then the second footman, then the third footman as they attended him at breakfast.

"And the same to you," said the Emperor merrily. He set to work opening all his birthday cards with one hand while he ate his porridge with the other. When the Emperor's porridge was finished, the Court Chamberlain beat the big brass gong that stood by the door. This was the signal for the pancakes. In came the fourth and fifth footmen bearing a large silver dish with a large silver cover. They marched up to the Emperor behind the Court Chamberlain.

"Happy Birthday, your Excellency," they all said together, bowing as low as possible.

"And the same to you," beamed the Emperor as he watched the Court Chamberlain remove the silver dish cover.

"Pancakes!" cried the Emperor, "How very nice! Capital!" – just as if he didn't have pancakes every day of the year. He watched as they were carefully lifted out onto his plate, one, two, three, four, five, each as round and crisp as ever. Then he stopped and stared and gasped as the sixth pancake was uncovered. Trembling with fury he slowly rose to his feet and roared just one word: "OBLONG!"

The terrified footmen turned tail and fled through the great bronze doors.

"OBLONG!" roared the Emperor again. "It's an insult! This pancake is oblong. Explain!" But the Court Chamberlain couldn't.

"I'll find out immediately, your . . . your . . . Excellency," he stammered, and with a hasty bow he hurried out through the great bronze doors.

Left to himself, the Emperor hurled the offending pancake out of the window and set about eating up the five round pancakes. Just as he was finishing, the Court Chamberlain hurried back.

"Excellency," he began, "Excellency, it would appear it was a birthday present."

The Emperor smiled. "I think I see," he said. "The frying pan was a birthday present and being oblong, it fried an oblong pancake."

Then he said, "You know, I rather like the idea of oblong pancakes. It's nice to be a little different isn't it?"

The Emperor was so pleased with the idea that he wished to share it with everyone in the Empire. Soon the whole population was buying oblong frying pans or banging round frying pans into an oblong shape.

But the Emperor's pleasure in his new discovery didn't stop there. He ordered oblong plates for his oblong pancakes, then oblong cups and saucers, oblong saucepans, oblong spoons, bottles and dishes; oblong hats, oblong umbrellas, even oblong wheels – which made travelling around most uncomfortable. Oblong apples and pears were more difficult. Farmers, gardeners, scientists and professors set to work on the problem. Soon every possible thing in the Empire was oblong.

Then one bright sunny day the Emperor looked up at the cloudless blue sky and he stopped . . . and he stared . . . and he gasped . . . and he roared – just one word: "ROUND!"

Everyone froze.

"ROUND!" roared the Emperor again. "The sun is round! It's ruining everything. Change it!"

This was more easily said than done, but the Court Chamberlain went off to try. He ordered the Emperor's woodmen to chop down all the trees and to build them into a tall, tall tower. Soon there were no more trees left and the sun seemed as far away as ever. The Court Chamberlain, the five footmen and the workers gave up.

"We have tried and tried and tried," they explained to

the furious Emperor. "We have done our best, Excellency."

"Your best is not good enough," said the Emperor crossly. "I shall do the job myself. Every evening the sun comes down to the edge of the earth. That is the time to deal with it."

He ordered his chariot and horses and, pressing his crown firmly on his head, shot away in a cloud of dust. It was many months before he returned, only to start off again in a new direction. This he did again and again until one day in spring he came back for the umpteenth time and summoned the people into the courtyard.

"My people," he said, "I have failed to reach the sun, but I have made a remarkable discovery. I have established through my many journeys and beyond all reasonable doubt an amazing scientific fact. The world is ROUND! It is round as round as round and very nice too. So now it is my wish that everything in the Empire should be round as well – to match."

The people were overjoyed because in all the time the Emperor had been away they had begun to tire of bumping about in carriages and carts with oblong wheels and had begun to change back to round ones. The hens were allowed to go back to laying round eggs and that meant round egg cups too. The gardeners had forgotten to use special fertilizers and the fruit trees began to produce ordinary round fruit.

The only things that didn't change back were the Emperor's pancakes. "I wouldn't like to hurt anyone's feelings," the Emperor said. "Besides, it's nice to be a little different after all!"

Adapted by Jean Gilbert from an original story by Peter Hughes

General notes

This humorous story relates immediately to shape and size, but apart from this obvious link with maths, it can also stimulate a number of other classroom activities.

1 Let the children retell the story. Discuss with them what kind of a man they think the Emperor was. We are not influenced by personal whims like the people in this story.

However, things do change from time to time, like fashion and coinage. Can the children think of any changes that sometimes affect our lives? Who is responsible for them?

2   Collect a number of utensils from home like egg whisks, mixing bowls, knives, forks, spoons. Discuss the suitability of their shapes and sizes. How many different shapes can the children find in specific groups like fruit, vegetables, boxes, windows?

3   Make two friezes to illustrate the story: a 'round' one and an 'oblong' one.

4   What words can the children associate with these two shapes? Round might be 'bubbly', 'circle', 'floating'. Oblong might be 'straight', 'bumpy', 'corners'. Can the children make sounds to go with each word? 'Bubbly' and 'bumpy' are straightforward, but the children will have to think more carefully about many of the other words. However, if you assemble a variety of different sound-makers – material, paper, sticks, stones – as well as a variety of instruments, it is surprising how many linking sounds the children will find. They can use their voices too!

5   Ask the children to compose some poems about round and oblong and use the ideas and words you have explored in (**4**). Let the children experiment with simple sound accompaniments. Divide them into groups to present their sound poems to one another, for example:

Balloons floating	Quiet glockenspiel
Bubbles glide and shimmer	Quiet glockenspiel
Red, red, evening sun	Cymbal tremolo
Round . . . sound . . . round	Voices humming

6   Ask the children to make designs or paint pictures about their poems.

7   See 'Dramatizing the story' on page 65.

Movement

Language and art can be a powerful stimulus to movement. Conversely, movement can enhance both language and art. Here are some suggestions that provide experiences in shape through movement.

1   Children walk on their own, tracing round/oblong shapes on the ground. They can skip or run as they move. They can go quickly or slowly. Use ropes if necessary to begin with, arranged to guide the movement.

2   Children trace round/oblong shapes in the air, using all the different spaces around them.

3   Children form round/oblong shapes with their bodies on the spot. Encourage them to use arms, legs, the top part of their bodies, their whole bodies, and to make their shapes horizontally, vertically, diagonally, kneeling or lying on the floor.

4   Do the same thing in groups of two, three or four.

5   Children run, walk, skip round/oblong shapes on their own. At a signal they freeze into a shape, which they can choose. Divide the class in half so that they can watch one another.

6   Pat a balloon in the air. Talk about the way it moves. The children dance like a balloon.

7 Similarly blow some bubbles. Observe and discuss the movement – contrast the smooth glide with the delicate burst as the bubbles disappear.

Now let the children create bubble dances, first of all moving on their own, then in groups. For group dances the children must think about the use of space and when each 'bubble' might burst. Let each group perform on their own.

Let the children work out some accompaniments. For example, two children could make gliding sounds on a xylophone or glockenspiel while a third could play a triangle or finger cymbal for each 'bubble' as it bursts.

8 This theme might inspire some of the children to choreograph a simple dance.

Small group (about eight children) Children are in a circle frozen into round shapes on the floor.	
One child in the centre mimes blowing bubbles.	Triangle or finger cymbal
The children slowly stand up and move gently round in a circle in round shapes.	Xylophone
They slowly break the circle and move round each other in pairs.	Glockenspiel
They break again and move on their own.	
One by one they 'burst' and sink to the ground.	Triangle or finger cymbal

9 Ask each child to bring in a flimsy nylon scarf. Use the ideas already outlined to create round/oblong dances. Here is a simple idea for an oblong group dance. This is possibly more difficult for younger children so it would help to have one child centred in the middle.

Small group dance for seven children

```
        O          O

   O         X          O

        O          O
```

Children sit with scarves in an oblong formation.	
The child in the centre improvises throughout.	
Children get up in stages, first kneeling, then standing, then bringing arms straight up over heads.	Triangle *for each stage*
Stepping back, they open arms and join hands to make a larger oblong. Stepping back again and dropping hands, they stretch out scarves in yet a larger oblong.	Cymbal *for each stage*
They break formation and dance on their own with scarves making straight/zigzag shapes at all levels.	Xylophone
They dance back to their original places holding scarves stretched high.	Cymbal
They bring arms down, kneel down, then sit down in reverse order as at the beginning.	Triangle

Musical activities

Although music cannot reflect shape for the children in the same way as movement, it can use the idea of shape to help structure their improvisations with both tuned and untuned percussion.

First introduce them to simple round

The Emperor's Oblong Pancake

singing. Start with easy songs that the children know well, for example: 'London's burning', 'Three blind mice', 'Frère Jacques', 'Row, row, row your boat' or 'Turn again Whittington'.

Make sure that the children can sing the tune easily without any help before introducing the round. They usually have a tendency to sing loudly in order to hear their own part, so keep first attempts quiet so that the different parts can hear one another. It is also necessary to keep together. This is easier if there is a leader for each group.

A round can go on and on, so there is always the question of how many times to sing through. Sing it once to make sure it works, then increase the repeats. A good number is three times and as the children become more experienced, musical interest can be maintained by varying the dynamics, getting louder as the round proceeds, or starting more quietly, getting louder and ending quietly.

Here are two rounds.

The Emperor's round

Japanese tune   Words by Jean Gilbert

Pan - cakes here,   pan - cakes there,

Pan - cakes ev' - ry - where.

Some for break - fast,   some for lunch, De -

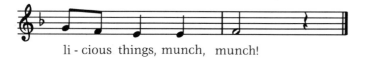

li - cious things, munch, munch!

Suggested accompaniment

Chime bars or glockenspiel

Something inside me

Words and music by Kenneth Simpson

Some-thing in - side me says, "Time for my tea,

Time for my tea,   Time for my tea!"

Suggested accompaniment

Tuned percussion

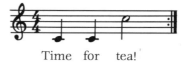

Time for tea!

Songs that go together

Some songs can be sung together because they have the same harmonic structure and melodic shapes that fit, rather like square, oblong or octagonal tiles that can be fitted into one another to make a pattern. The children will be intrigued by the resultant rhythmic and harmonic patterns when they do this. Here is a simple example to try, which recorders can play as well:

Pease pudding hot

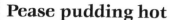

Further examples of songs that go together can be found in the following:

Flying a Round ed. Gadsby and Harrop (A & C Black, 1982)

Mix 'n' Match (Instant Part Singing) David Jenkins and Mark Visocchi (Universal Edition (London) Ltd, 1977) (UE 16136 L)

Tops and Tails, Eight Children's Songs arranged by Anne Mendoza (Oxford University Press, 1968)

Improvising and ensemble playing

An approach to this aspect of music making can be found on pages 10–12 of the 'Introduction'. An outline of simple shape in music is given in the section on 'Sound pictures' on page 9.

Rondo form

This is a piece of music that has a recurring section rather like the chorus of a song. Thus the shape will be A B A C A D A, and so on.

If your children are ready for simple ensemble playing, show them how to make up a piece in this form.

1 You will need four tuned instruments. If there are more, they can double up; if less, shorten the rondo or let the children share instruments.

2 Remove the notes F and B so that the notes of the pentatonic C scale remain: C D E G A C, or as many notes as the children have learnt to use.

3 Let the children agree upon the main repeating section. It is easiest to base this upon the word rhythms of a short rhyme which could be linked with the story, for example:

I like pancakes,
Nothing else will do.
Pancakes for breakfast
And all the day through.

The Emperor's Oblong Pancake

4 Choose another rhyme of similar length, such as 'Pease pudding hot' or 'Mix a pancake', for the other sections. Let all the children have a turn at making up a tune to these word rhythms. Choose three different versions. It doesn't matter if the children cannot remember their tunes note for note, so long as they can join in the final play-through and keep going.

5 Now play right through in the rondo form. It will probably need several attempts before the children can play through rhythmically without gaps between each section, but as with everything else, practice makes perfect, and the more time the children have to experiment on their own, the better.

6 Some children will be ready to add accompaniments to each section (see Introduction, pages 10–12). Start with just one simple accompaniment like a one-note drone and build up according to the success of what has been achieved and enjoyed by the children.

Country dancing

Most of our singing games use the form of a circle or two straight lines and can lead directly into simple country dancing. The following dances are good examples of circle and longways formations and are easy ones to start with.

Elsden circle dance

Tune: 'Miss Bennet's jig'

B

Children take partners, join hands and form a circle.

A1 Circle left, skipping or side-stepping.

A2 Circle right.

B1 Swing partners: join hands and skip round on the spot.

B2 Promenade: children on the inside lead partners round in a circle. Just before the end they move up one place and the dance begins again with new partners.

Oxo reel

Tune: 'The muffin man'

A

Swedish clap dance

Children take partners and form a longways set of six on each side.

A1 Joining hands in lines, children go forward and back once. Drop hands, do a right-hand turn with partner and go back to places.

A2 Repeat, but this time do a left-hand turn with partner.

B1 Top and bottom couples circle left, then right, while middle four couples do a right-hand then a left-hand 'star', by joining right hands in the centre and skipping clockwise, dropping hands, then joining left hands in the centre and skipping anticlockwise.

B2 Top couple swings to the bottom of the set. Everyone claps in time to the music.

The dance proceeds until the original top couple is back in place.

This dance can be done as a single partner dance first, to concentrate on the movements. Any number of couples can be grouped into a circle; six to eight couples is about right.

A1 Partners skip round in a circle, holding hands. (The step for older children is a forward polka starting on the outside foot. Hands swing backwards and forwards with each step.)

B1 Drop hands and face partner. Bow/curtsey and clap three times. Repeat. Clap own hands, clap partner's hands twice. Turn on the spot and stamp three times.

A2 Repeat **A1**.

B2 As for **B1** except for clapping. Instead, shake fingers at one another, first one hand, then the other.

The Emperor's Oblong Pancake

Bow Belinda   Virginian singing game

1 Bow, bow, bow Be-lin-da,

Bow, bow, bow Be-lin-da, Bow, bow,

bow Be-lin-da, Won't you be my part-ner?

2 Right hand round, Belinda . . .

3 Left hand round, Belinda . . .

4 Both hands round, Belinda . . .

5 Lead couple down, Belinda . . .

6 Follow the leader round, Belinda . . .

7 Under the arch and back to your places . . .

Children take partners and form two lines. Eight couples is a good number. They can sing as they dance; the words help. Start by teaching the first four movements and add the rest when the first part is well established.

1 Couples face one another, six steps apart. They take three steps forward, bow and step three paces back.

2 Couples step forward to meet, circle with right hands, then step back.

3 Repeat with left hands.

4 Repeat with both hands.

5 Lead couple skip or walk down the inside of the set, then back again to their places. Everyone claps.

6 Everyone turns to face the top of the set and each line follows the top child who turns outwards and back down to the bottom of the set to form an arch.

7 Partners join one another as they go under the arch back to their places – except the lead couple who remain at the bottom.

The dance continues until the original lead couple find themselves back at the top again.

Making up dances

Once the children have learnt a few basic movements they could go on to make up their own group dances to tunes that they know, for example:

Circle dance to tune of 'Pop goes the weasel' (not too fast)

Half a pound of tuppenny rice,	
Half a pound of treacle,	*Circle left*
That's the way the money goes –	*Circle right*
Pop goes the weasel!	*Clapping*
Up and down the City Road,	*Steps into the centre*
In and out the Eagle,	*Steps out again*
That's the way the money goes –	*Skip round*
Pop goes the weasel!	*and clap*

There are 15 simple dances outlined in *Country Dancing* plus a cassette of the tunes (Scholastic Publications Ltd, 9 Parade, Leamington Spa, Warwickshire CV32 4DG).

Dramatizing the story

Characters

Emperor
Court Chamberlain
Five footmen
Courtiers
Workers
People
Group of musicians and singers
Dancers
Narrator

Narrator introduces the play.
The Emperor's Round is sung by everyone.

Scene 1 Inside the Emperor's palace	Dances and songs
Enter Emperor, looking pleased as it is his birthday. *A gong sounds.* Dancers come in, greet the Emperor and dance.	*Elsden circle dance*
Emperor sits down to breakfast.	
Footmen bring breakfast and birthday cards, greet Emperor. *Gong sounds.*	
Pancakes are ceremoniously brought in.	
Emperor finds oblong pancake.	*Pancake song, verse 1*
He finds out the reason for the oblong pancake and orders a general move from round to oblong shapes.	*Pancake song, verse 2*

Scene 2   Outside the Emperor's palace

A busy scene with people coming and going, handling as many oblong objects as possible. Conversation centres around the new shape.	
Some dancers enter announcing their new, oblong dance.	*Oxo reel/ Bow Belinda*
Enter Emperor. He sees that the sun is round.	*Pancake song, verse 3*
Court Chamberlain orders workers to build a high tower so as to reach the sun. They go off.	*Repeat verse 3*
They return, unsuccessful. Emperor summons his chariot. *Gong sounds.* He announces that he will deal with the sun and goes off. Everyone cheers.	
They sing chorus of song as they walk off.	*Repeat chorus*

Scene 3   Outside the Emperor's palace

A year has passed. A few gardeners are looking at the round fruit growing on the trees and commenting on the problems of growing oblong fruit. *A gong sounds.* The Emperor returns looking excited but the worse for wear. He summons the Court Chamberlain and orders him to call an important meeting. *Gong sounds.* People and workers enter. Emperor tells the people of his discovery.	*Pancake song, verse 4*
Everyone is delighted to get back to normal. Children come in playing with hoops and beach balls. Everyone joins in a round dance.	*Elsden circle dance*

Music for listening and moving

If required, excerpts from any suitably festive music can be used since the story is not 'set' in any particular country. Excerpts from *Façade* by William Walton would provide a humorous or jaunty sound. To complement an oriental setting, excerpts from Britten's *Prince of the Pagodas* could be used.

The oblong pancake song

Words and music by Jane Morgan

square, it's not round, But it's ob-long.____ No, not

e-ven a pent-a-gon, No, not e-ven a hex-a-gon, No, not

e-ven an oct-a-gon, Or a do-do-do-do-do-dec-a-gon! It's not

The Emperor's Oblong Pancake

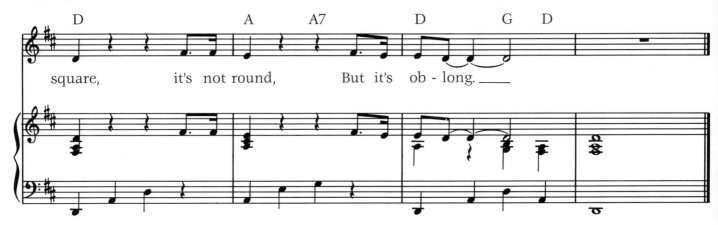

square,   it's not round,   But it's ob - long. _____

Note Clap two crotchet claps in the rests of the chorus: It's not square ♩ ♩ etc.

2 Oblong pancakes! What a good idea!
We could use some changes around here,
Oblong cups and saucers, plates and
spoons,
All things will be oblong very soon.

CHORUS
They won't be square, they won't be round,
But they'll be oblong.
They won't be square, they won't be round,
But they'll be oblong.
No, not even a pentagon . . .

3 What is this I see up in the sky?
This round, golden sun offends my eye.
Build a tall, tall tower from my trees,
Change that sphere to oblong, if you please.

CHORUS
It shouldn't be square, it shouldn't be round,
It should be oblong.
It shouldn't be square, it shouldn't be round,
It should be oblong.
No, not even a pentagon . . .

4 In my travels round the world I found
To my great amazement, this world's round.
Make your objects round is my decree,
All except my pancake made for me.

CHORUS
It's not square, it's not round,
But it's oblong.
It's not square, it's not round,
But it's oblong.
No, not even a pentagon . . .

The Fairy at the Fair

Long ago a man named Thomas lived with his wife Betsy at Netherwitton in Northumberland. Every year they gave themselves a treat by walking to Longhorsley Fair: five miles there, and five miles back, and well worth every step of the way – except for one thing. Each year they wished, even more than the year before, that they had a child to enjoy the Fair with them. But no child was ever born to them.

One year, the day after they had been to the Fair, there came a loud 'Rat-a-tat-tat' on their door. Outside was a man, a woman and a merry little lad.

Thomas bade them welcome, inviting them to step inside.

"I saw you yesterday at the Fair," the man explained. "I was looking for someone to look after our boy for a time, maybe for two years – or more. As you looked a kindly couple I made enquiries throughout the neighbourhood and learned where you lived, and that you had no children of your own. So we wonder if you would be willing to foster young Hobbie if we pay you well for your trouble, and if we fetch him home again when the time comes."

Betsy and Thomas were delighted with the offer, for Hobbie seemed at home with them straight away.

Before he left, the father handed Betsy a large jar of ointment, saying: "This is for Hobbie's eyes. Every night you must smear a little on both his eyes. Whatever happens, do *not* use it on your own eyes, or you will be in great trouble!"

The foster parents promised readily. It seemed a simple enough instruction to follow.

Hobbie proved to be a very happy boy, full of goodness and badness, tricks, mischief, and high spirits, so that it never occurred to Thomas or Betsy that he was anything other than an ordinary mortal boy. He grew and thrived, and each night Betsy anointed his eyes just as she had been told, till the time came round again for Longhorsley Fair.

Now all through that year, Thomas, who was more inquisitive than his wife, had been puzzling over the strange ban on the ointment. The night before the Fair his curiosity got the better of him, and while the other two were asleep he spread some on his own left eye, and what do you think happened then? Nothing at all! He could see neither better nor worse than before.

"So that's all right," he said to himself, "Just a silly fuss over nowt!"

The next morning they set off for the Fair. So that Hobbie's short legs would not wear out before they got there, Thomas popped him into a wheelbarrow, and as he was trundled along Betsy told him all about the animals, and the peep-shows, and the coconut-shies, and everything else there would be at the end of their journey.

When they reached Longhorsley, Hobbie could hardly wait to be tipped out of the barrow, so excited was he to see and hear all that was going on.

He heard the toot-tootle-toot and the tap-tap-tap of the pipe and tabor playing for the sword-dancers and the morris-men; the tink-tinkle-tink of the little bells hanging from their garters; and the fiddle-diddle-dee of the fiddlers playing for the country dancing on the green. Betsy and Thomas joined in that, but Hobbie joined in everything. He stamped and jumped and twisted with the morris-men; he turned somersaults and cartwheels on the edge of the crowd watching the acrobats and jugglers; he threw crab-apples high in the air and tried to catch them, but generally missed. He clapped louder than anyone else at the wrestling and the mummer's play. He stroked horses that neighed, patted cows that mooed and sheep that bleated, and scratched pigs that grunted with his little pointed stick.

Then they wandered among the booths searching for a small fairing, some toy for Hobbie to take home with him.

Suddenly Thomas nudged Betsy.

"Look there!" he whispered, pointing to a booth where butter and cheese were on sale. "Hobbie's father! He's stealing cheese, and no one's stopping him!"

"I see nothing," said Betsy. "You must be drunk, or dreaming!"

But Thomas followed the man around the Fair, and everywhere he stole a little something, yet no one but Thomas seemed able to see him.

Finally Thomas tapped him on the shoulder and said: "Good-day to you! You seem to be helping yourself very generously."

The man turned on him angrily: "Which eye do you see me with?" he snarled.

"With this one," said Thomas, pointing to the one he had smeared with ointment.

"Meddlesome mortal! Take that then!" said the Fairy Man, for a fairy he certainly was, and he blew gently on Thomas's left eye.

What happened after that is something of a puzzle. Even new tales, and especially old ones, change a little from one telling to the next, according to who is doing the telling. But one thing is certain. Inquisitive Thomas never again saw anything that the fairies didn't want him to see. He didn't even see Hobbie any more, but then neither did Betsy or anyone else in Northumberland. He must have gone back to the Fairy People where he belonged, and it is my guess that Thomas and Betsy found a little human boy in need of a good home, to look after in his place.

Kathleen Hersom

General notes

In many parts of the country, fairs are an integral part of the life of an area, some of them dating as far back as medieval times when merchants travelled from other countries and pedlars came from outlying districts to sell their wares. More recently, especially in urban areas, fairs are often permanently sited and somewhat commercial. Whatever the nature of the local fair, the excitement, colour and magic still appeal to children of all ages.

The following suggested classroom activities can be adapted for specific age groups.

1 The story, set in the past in Northumberland, has all the nuances of the traditional folk tale. The whys and wherefores of fairy doings defy reason and explanation, but the children may well question the puzzle of Thomas's encounter with the Fairy Man at the fair and the disappearance of Hobbie. They may think

of another ending to the story. What kind of fair was the one at Longhorsley? What kinds of things did Hobbie enjoy at the fair?

2   Talk about visits that the children have made to fairs. What kinds of things did they enjoy?

3   Ask the children to write about a visit to a fair, or to invent an imaginary adventure story about a fair, or to retell 'The Fairy at the Fair' in their own words.

4   Some children could find out about the history of fairs and markets. Make a collection of suitable information and picture books.

5   Build up a colourful frieze from the children's paintings and/or cutouts. These could be made in the form of a collage.

6   As a craft and science activity, make working models of swings, roundabouts, a big wheel and a helter-skelter.

7   Set up stalls and sideshows according to available space and extent of class involvement. Activities could include working with money and playing games like guessing the weight of the cake or the number of sweets in a jar; measuring time with the aid of an egg-timer or stop-watch; bingo; hoop-la; and maths activities like sorting balloons into colour, shape and size.

Movement

Much of this can be built around the movement of the roundabout and swing-type amusements, while a more general approach involving the activities of people at a fair could introduce drama and mime.

Swings

Children swing arms high-low-high across bodies, legs apart and knees bending for swing. Start with small swings, getting bigger, then smaller again.

Swing-boats

Children sit on the floor in pairs facing each other, with hands joined and legs tucked up. They pull forward and back with controlled movements, these movements getting bigger, then smaller again.

Roundabouts

Children glide round on their own, imitating the up and down galloping movements of the traditional roundabout horses. They practise going quickly and slowly. Turn the whole class into a roundabout with the children in concentric circles. They must be aware of space and relate to the movement of others; they will be going up and down at different times. (Recorded music can be played if required.)

Big wheel

Children turn their bodies into a big wheel, straight arms stretched high and making as large a circle as possible, high, wide and low. The movement must be steady but can get faster, then slower as the 'ride' finishes.

Big dipper

Children travel around on their own, making graduated high and low movements as they go. Movements going 'downhill' will be slightly faster, but great control is needed.

Helter-skelter

Children indicate the downward, spiralling movement with their bodies, arms outstretched. The journey from the top to the bottom can be quite long, so the movement can be broad, graduated and controlled.

The fairground

Let the children work in small groups to devise a pattern of movement. Recorded music could be played to encourage some ideas. Each child can portray a different machine, stopping and starting at different times. It may be necessary to limit these to, say, three to start with. The children could start or finish with the roundabout, when each child could be one of the horses.

Generally these movements are best done unaccompanied, although a short, recorded excerpt (see 'Music for listening and moving', page 77) would give atmosphere to the roundabouts and fairground.

Mime

To get the feel of the bustle and excitement of a fair, start with a piece of music that sets the scene. The beginning of Stravinsky's ballet music *Petrushka* evokes a wonderful picture of a fairground crowd. The story should captivate any child. It is about a puppet master, who is a magician, and his three puppets – Petrushka, the Blackamoor and the Ballerina. The music portrays the great square of St Petersburg in holiday mood on a Shrove Tuesday, but it could equally well describe a holiday fairground in this country.

The children could mime different characters: stallholders attracting customers, passers-by, musicians or a parading band, an organ grinder, a group of clowns or acrobats, even the puppet master in the Petrushka story setting up his theatre. The children could work out some group scenes around the various centres of attraction, culminating in a larger group as they drift towards the puppet theatre or the acrobats.

Musical activities

Sound picture

Ask the children to work out sound impressions of the movement of the various amusements. Here are some suggestions.

Sound source	Suggested sounds
Swings	Swanee whistle (up and down)
Swing-boats	Xylophone – random notes from word rhythm 'to and fro' or short glides
Roundabouts	Shakers (round and round) Three or four chime bars played in continuous sequence
Big wheel	Deep-sounding tambour – scratched or continuous beat
Big dipper	Metallophone – big and small slides up and down
Helter-skelter	Alto xylophone – slow-moving slide from high to low notes

Work out some fairground cries like 'Come and buy a coloured balloon' and 'Roll up, roll up, roll up, come and have a go'. Accompany with an occasional noisy sound from a rattle, if you have one, or a guiro.

The arrangement

This could begin with several fair cries, then the sound of the various amusements could come and go in a sequence decided by the children. This could build up to a big sound with everyone joining in, or the sequence could continue, giving the impression of drifting through the fairground.

Fair cries

The calls and cries of the stallholders can be a good starting-point for language work. Here is a traditional street cry:

Giddy girls and noisy boys,
Come and buy my painted toys.
Medals made of ginger bread
And penny horses white and red.

There is also the well known 'Cherry ripe, cherry ripe . . .'. Both these cries can be found in *Strawberry Fair* by Carol Tate (Collins, 1973).

The children can compare these cries with ones they may have heard at fairs. They could make up their own cries which could be linked with any stalls set up in the classroom. Encourage them to make up simple tunes for their cries (see 'Introduction' page 10), for example:

Using notes D E G A

Ask volunteers to teach their tunes to the rest of the class. Select a few – four or more according to the children's previous experience – and get the other children to learn them. Prepare cards with the words only. Try these games:

The Fairy at the Fair

1 The children sit in a circle around a box containing the cards. They pass a bean bag round while they chant:

> Round and round the fairground,
> Which one shall I try?
> Round and round the fairground,
> Listen to the cry.

Whoever has the bean bag on the word 'cry' picks a card from the box, then tries to remember the tune. He/she can ask the 'composer' for help if necessary. Everyone sings. The game continues.

2 Divide the children into groups and give them each a cry to sing. Play one of the cries on the chimes or hum the tune and see how quickly the correct group can recognize and sing it.

Making up tunes

(See Introduction page 10.) Encourage the children to make up their own fairground song. They could 'set' a verse of their own or compose a tune using the word rhythms from a simple poem, for example:

> I've seen caravans
> Going to the fair!
> Come along,
> Come along,
> Let's go there!
>
> *from 'Caravans' by Irene Thompson*

> Riding horses, swinging high,
> Helter skelter round we fly.
> Flashing lights and noise and bustle,
> Laughing crowds all in a hustle.
>
> *from 'The fair' by E. M. Stanton*

The full version of both these poems can be found in *Seeing and Doing* ed. Rosalind Farrimond (Thames Television, 1985).

Using notes C E G A C'

I've seen ca-ra-vans go-ing to the fair!

Come a-long, come a-long, Let's go there!

Add a drone and a percussion accompaniment:

DRONE

TAMBOURINE

(go - ing to the fair)

Music for listening and moving

Fairground Organs (Thursford Collection OU 2228)
No longer current but available from local libraries.

Gaudin Fair Organ
1 'All the fun of the fair' (Record: Joys 168; Cassette: Joys 217)
2 'Come to the fair' (Record: Joys 167; Cassette: Joys 216)

Holiday Sound Effects (BBC REC 301)
Section on funfairs and seaside has sounds for roundabouts, atmosphere, machines . . .

Petrushka (short excerpt from beginning) Stravinsky

The fun of the fair

Czech singing game
Arranged by **Sidney Northcote**
English words by 'E. L.'

Gaily

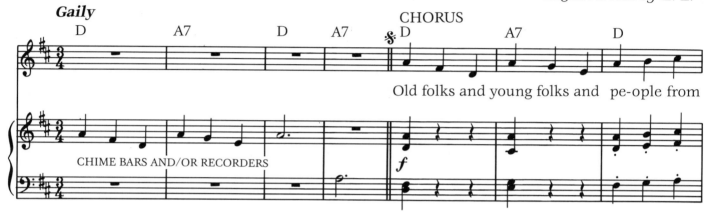

Old folks and young folks and pe-ople from

ev - 'ry - where, Hust - ling and bust - ling, They've come to the fair.

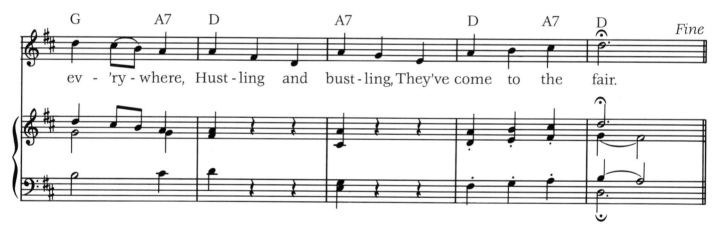

A little slower

VERSE

(*The pedlar*)
1 See how my tray is lad - en, With rings for a man or mai - den; And

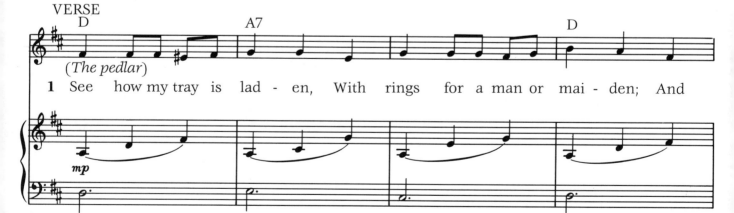

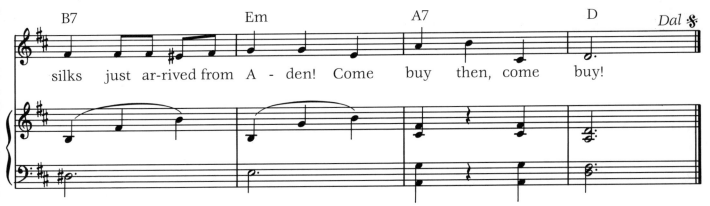

(*The fortune teller*)

2 Give me a silver shilling,
   To bring you good luck I'm willing,
   And tell you a fortune thrilling!
   Come try then, come try!

   CHORUS Old folks and young folks, etc.

This is a song about an old-fashioned fair like the one at Longhorsley. Ask the children to make up some verses about Hobbie's visit to the fair.

Suggested percussion

Chorus

TAMBOURINE

Recorders could accompany the chorus as well.

Verse

TRIANGLE

The Fairy at the Fair

The fairground

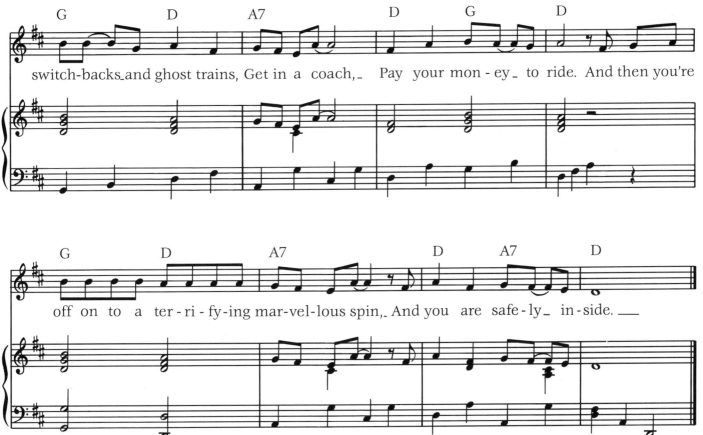

switch-backs and ghost trains, Get in a coach,_ Pay your mon - ey_ to ride. And then you're

off on to a ter - ri - fy-ing mar-vel-lous spin,_ And you are safe - ly_ in-side. ___

CHORUS   Hear the band play, etc.

2   And there are horses for riding
Round and around,
Each one ready to go,
And as they gallop faster through the air,
the higher you swing,
See the people below.

CHORUS   Hear the band play, etc.

3   Let's go on swing boats a-sailing
Up in the sky
Dipping nearly upside down.
Then find the tower for the helter-skelter –
climb to the top,
Then spin, spin down to the ground.

CHORUS   Hear the band play, etc.

4   You'll like the sideshows with pop guns,
Rifles and rings,
Win a big teddy bear;
And we'll buy candyfloss and lollipops and
burgers and chips,
It's all there down at the fair.

CHORUS   Hear the band play, etc.

This song describes the noise and excitement
of a modern fairground. The speed of the
opening chorus should be steady enough to
enable the children to sing easily all the words
of the verses, especially the fourth line.

Suggested percussion

Chorus

CHIME BARS/RECORDERS

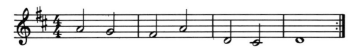

DRUM AND CYMBAL

(cymbal)

Verses

These can be sung unaccompanied unless the children wish to suggest instruments like a coconut or wood blocks for the horses in verse 2.

There are suggestions on the cassette that accompanies this book.

Movement

The tune lends itself to movement or a simple group dance. Here are some suggestions:

Chorus

March round to the beat. Clap after the word 'town' and change direction. Adjust the speed to the children's movement. Accompany with drum and cymbal as suggested for the song.

Verses

Improvise movement patterns with the children moving on their own, with partners or in groups (see 'Movement' notes, pages 74–75). Accompany with suitable percussion according to suggestions from the children.

Dance

Chorus

Children march round in a ring, holding hands. Clap after the word 'town' and change direction.

Verse 1

Children circle round with a partner, right hands across, then left hands, changing direction.

Verse 2

Move round in a circle as for a roundabout.

Verse 3

Swing arms to and fro, facing a partner, then spin round on the spot.

Verse 4

Drop hands and face the middle. Take three steps out, clap, then three steps back to the centre. Join hands with partner and swing for the last two lines.

Stone Soup

Many years ago there lived a poor beggar. He could find no work anywhere and spent his days wandering about the countryside begging for food and money wherever he went.

One day, late in the afternoon, he found himself near a large mansion. As he was tired and hungry, he thought that this seemed a likely place to find food and shelter for the night. So he made his way to the kitchen quarters, where the servants lived, and knocked at the door. A serving-maid came to see who it was.

"And what is it you want?" she demanded. "You are too dirty to come into the house, and if it is food that you want – we have nothing to give you at all."

"Well, I am sorry about that," replied the poor beggar, who stooped down to pick up a stone from the ground.

"Don't throw that at me!" shrieked the maid. "May the good Lord have mercy on us."

"I hope you find Him merciful," said the man. "Then, perhaps you in your turn will have mercy on me. All I need is a little water and a pan to put it in. Then I will boil the water and make some soup out of this stone."

The footman, who had been listening, asked him to stay for an hour or so. He was curious to find out how this 'stone soup' was made, for he had never heard of such a thing. He sent for a pan of water, and when the other servants heard what this was for, they came crowding out into the courtyard to laugh and poke fun at the visitor.

The beggar took no notice at all. He lit a fire with some sticks and dry grass, washed the stone, put the stone carefully into the water and set the pan over the fire to boil. The serving-maid made fun of him, giving him a spoon with a long wooden handle.

The man thanked her. "You have been kind enough to lend me these cooking utensils and to give me some water. Perhaps, now, you could let me have some salt and pepper so that I can season the soup."

One of the servants fetched the salt and pepper. The

man thanked him, tipped some into the water and stirred until the salt had dissolved. Then he tasted the liquid.

"Mm – this tastes quite good already. But it would taste even better if I added a few scraps of meat."

Another servant went to the kitchen and returned with a basin full of meat scraps. The man thanked her, added these to the pan of water and let everything simmer and bubble away on the fire for a few minutes. Then he tasted it again.

"Ah, delicious!" he cried. "But it would taste even better if I added some left-over vegetable pieces."

These were also fetched and dropped straight away into the pot. The curious servants watched the beggar as he stirred away and then tasted the 'soup'.

"How splendid this soup is becoming, and how delicious the flavouring of the stone. But still, these scraps have made a difference and the flavour would be even better if I added a little sauce. Have you any to spare, my friends?"

This time it was the serving-maid who went to fetch the sauce. The beggar thanked her kindly and spooned the sauce into the soup. Then he stirred it slowly and watched it as it simmered merrily over the fire.

"Excellent," he said after the final taste. "Never before have I tasted a better stone soup."

"Let us taste too," cried the serving-maid. Everyone wanted to taste the soup, for they still did not quite believe that soup could be made from a stone.

"It is delicious," said one.

"Really excellent," said another.

"The best stone soup that anyone could make," said a third.

"We must make some for ourselves," said a fourth. "The beggar has certainly taught us something new. Perhaps we should let him sleep in the barn tonight."

Having agreed to let the beggar stay the night, the servants went back to the kitchen to prepare the dinner for their master and his family.

The beggar stayed by the fire where he sipped his excellent stone soup. Then he went across to the barn, covered himself with hay and fell sound asleep.

Traditional folk tale retold by Jean Gilbert

General notes

Suggested classroom activites for slightly older children are as follows:

1 Ask questions about the story.
How did the politeness of the beggar help him to get a meal and a bed for the night? Why did the servants help him to prepare the soup? What finally persuaded them to let him stay the night?

2 Encourage the children to retell the story. Individual children could relate the various episodes, keeping to the sequence of events in the story.

3 The children could write and illustrate their own stories or contribute to a class story book.

4 Make a frieze entitled 'How to make stone soup'.

5 The story might lead to a discussion on unemployment, the ways in which families try to manage when there are no regular wages coming in, and the effects on people of being unemployed.

6 Make a class book of simple recipes that the children enjoy.

7 If practical, ask the children to bring in a sample of their favourite soup. Organize a tasting session. Can the children guess any of the ingredients? They should know what the ingredients of their own samples are. List these for checking the guesses.

Movement

The characters

The beggar

Ask the children to describe what kind of a man he might be – old, young, bearded, obviously not fat? How would he walk and move at the end of a long, weary day? Let each child interpret his/her own ideas of the man wandering, begging for food, looking for a place to spend the night.

The serving-maid

Talk about the kind of girl she might be. What was her attitude to the stranger at the door, for instance? The children can improvise the various jobs she might do in the kitchen and the way she might serve the meals at table.

The footman

How would the children interpret this character? He was certainly curious enough about the stone soup to ask the beggar to stay, and to send for some water and a pan. What would be his duties in the big mansion?

The other servants

Let the children decide on a specific character and interpret a variety of jobs.

Divide the children into groups. Each group decides which child will play each character. The group then prepares a movement sequence to represent the hurry and bustle inside the big kitchen, then the surprise knock at the door and the build-up of events leading to the cooking of the beggar's stone soup.

Stone Soup

Cooking

This involves all the movements to do with handling food, the qualities of the ingredients and the texture of things like bread dough and cake mixture. It could be amusing to accompany the movements with sound effects. Suggestions for these are included below.

Movements	Suggested sound effects
Weighing Pouring, placing in scales, looking at weight	Triangle – trill for pouring, strike for placing and noting weight
Grating Slow and quick grating	Guiro
Breaking eggs Holding and tapping egg, opening shell, watching egg slide out	Xylophone – high note glissando from high to low
Pouring into bowl Gently tipping container, tapping, scraping to empty it	Shaker
Mixing Slow mix to start with, turning bowl, getting quicker	Sand block
Beating Hold bowl with one hand, beating movements with the other	Triangle trill
Whisking Very quick controlled movements with whisking hand staying in one place	Egg whisk
Kneading Strong hand movement feeling texture of dough	Tambour tapped and/or scraped
Cutting/chopping Children decide what they are cutting/chopping and at what speed they work	Wood block

The children will suggest other things to do and how they could be accompanied.

These ideas can now form the basis of some movement sequences.

1 If the children have done any cooking at school, ask them to describe exactly what they did, then let them mime some or all of their activities (best without accompaniment).

2 Ask the children to suggest several short sequences, such as:

weighing fat, sugar, then blending and beating mixture;

cracking several eggs, then beating them;

cutting up vegetables, putting them in water in a saucepan, seasoning, putting on stove to cook.

Practise these sequences, then ask a volunteer to mime one of them. Whoever guesses correctly does the next mime.

3 Television cook-in

The idea is to present a television cookery programme for children. This could be either serious or comic with the children working in small groups of one or two presenters and several musicians to provide sound effects.

Musical activities

Word rhythm games

Make cards for food with different word rhythms, for example:

		Claps
Soup	♩	* *hold*
Carrot	♫	* *
Cauliflow'r	♫ ♩	* * *

The cards could have pictures or words on the front with the claps or music notes on the back.

Practise saying and clapping them all. When the children have learnt the rhythm associated with each card, play some of the games outlined in the unit entitled 'Lucy Ladybird'.

Here are some more ideas:

Build up sequences based on the word rhythms of different food groups, for example:

Spring greens cau-li-flow'r car-rot leek

Optional arrangements

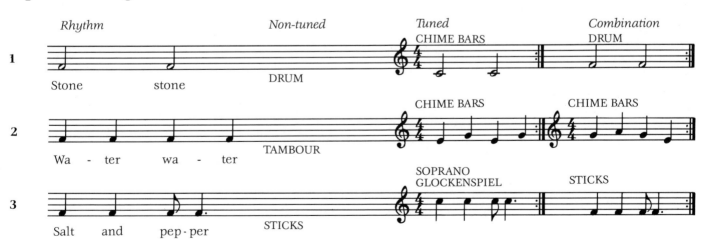

(♩ ♩ ♪♩ ♫ ♩ ♫ ♩ ♩)
Pear black-ber-ry pine-ap-ple plum

(♫ ♩ ♪♩. ♩ ♫ ♩ ♩)
Coo-king fat but-ter mar-ga-rine oil

Learn the rhythms of the phrases and then add combinations of different body sounds to each phrase, for example clapping, tapping, finger clicking, knee slapping.

Divide the children into groups and let them work out a pattern of rhythmic sounds for their phrases. Ask each group to perform their piece several times through. Can two/three groups play together? Keep the pulse going with a drum or tambour.

Musical soup

Use the soup cooking sequence as a basis for simple ensemble playing based on word rhythms from the story (see Introduction, pages 10–12). The idea is to start with one instrument and build up until all instruments are playing together. Both tuned and untuned instruments can be used in any combination.

 *Stone Soup*

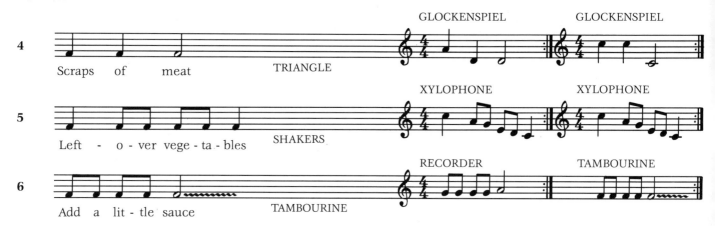

4 Scraps of meat — TRIANGLE — GLOCKENSPIEL — GLOCKENSPIEL

5 Left - o - ver vege - ta - bles — SHAKERS — XYLOPHONE — XYLOPHONE

6 Add a lit - tle sauce — TAMBOURINE — RECORDER — TAMBOURINE

Decide how many times each instrument plays before the next one begins. Make some 'stirring' sounds between each entry. Ask the children how they could end their composition. For instance, a cymbal might sound to suggest that the soup is cooked.

Poems

Breakfast

Sausages, sausages sizzling in the pan;
Eggs flipping and a-flopping,
Catch them if you can!

Porridge, porridge bubbling on the stove,
Slurping and a-glurping,
That's the food I love!

Bacon crinkling, wrinkling at the edges;
Toast browning and a-burning,
Popping out the toaster
In great fat wedges!

Tangy, bitter marmalade
With chewy chunks of peel.
That's the breakfast that I like –
The day's best meal!

Adrian Rumble

Mustard

I'm mad about mustard –
Even on custard.

Ogden Nash

Spaghetti

Spaghetti, spaghetti, all over the place,
Up to my elbows – up to my face,
Over the carpet and under the chairs,
Into the hammock and wound round the stairs,
Filling the bathtub and covering the desk,
Making the sofa a mad mushy mess.

The party is ruined, I'm terribly worried,
The guests have all left (unless they're all buried).
I told them, "Bring presents." I said, "Throw confetti."
I guess they heard wrong
'Cause they all threw spaghetti!

Shel Silverstein

Ask the children to make up verses about their favourite meal, or even a couplet exploiting rhyming food names.

Salt, mustard, vinegar, pepper

Based on a skipping chant arranged by Anne Mendoza and Joan Rimmer

Stone Soup

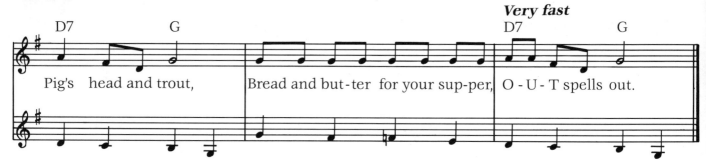

Pig's head and trout, | Bread and but-ter for your sup-per, | O - U - T spells out.

Play G6 with G on sixth string and first three strings open.

Salt, mustard, vinegar, pepper

This skipping chant should be sung quite fast and requires careful singing with very clear words. The children might like to reword it, using their own food phrases.

The accompaniment can be played on any tuned percussion, the piano or treble recorder. It can be divided between two or four players:

FIRST TUNE

Second player on the repeat

SECOND TUNE

Third player

Fourth player

The melody lies within the range of the descant recorder. An ensemble arrangement could be made involving the piano, recorder and tuned percussion.

One ginger beer

These three songs can be sung simultaneously by three different groups. Begin by learning the first two tunes and dividing the children into two groups. Do the same with the second and third tunes. Sing all three together as and when the children are ready. Choose leaders for each group.

If the children have difficulty in starting together, ask the first group to sing their song once through first, then add the second group. When the first group has sung their song twice through, bring in the third group. Decide how many times to sing through all together and how to end: loudly, quietly, with a slight *rallentando* or slowing down, or with the songs stopping one by one.

One ginger beer

Clearly; not too fast

Traditional rhyme collected by Alison McMorland

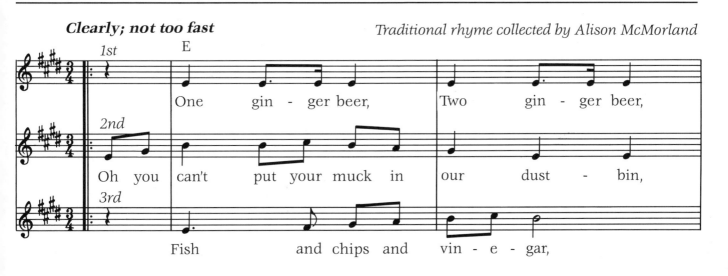

1st — E

One gin - ger beer, Two gin - ger beer,

2nd

Oh you can't put your muck in our dust - bin,

3rd

Fish and chips and vin - e - gar,

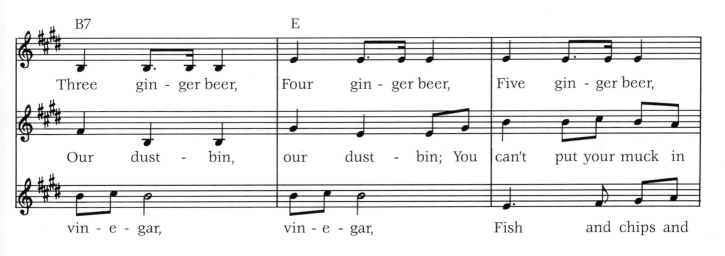

B7 — E

Three gin - ger beer, Four gin - ger beer, Five gin - ger beer,

Our dust - bin, our dust - bin; You can't put your muck in

vin - e - gar, vin - e - gar, Fish and chips and

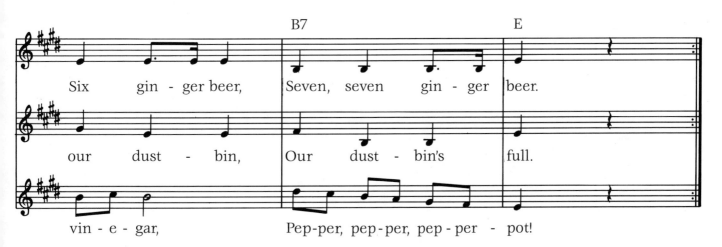

B7 — E

Six gin - ger beer, Seven, seven gin - ger beer.

our dust - bin, Our dust - bin's full.

vin - e - gar, Pep-per, pep-per, pep-per - pot!

Professor Noah's Spaceship

Once upon a time there was a huge forest, and all kinds of animals and birds lived happily there.

As the years passed, the forest began to change. The air around it started to smell and turned a nasty colour. No longer did the sunlight filter through the leaves. The leaves started to fall from the trees, and their fruit began to turn bad.

A strange sadness came over the forest. The animals were bewildered. They became so desperate that the Lion, the king of beasts, decided to call a meeting of all animals and birds. "What's happening to our forest?" they all cried.

"The air is so foul that when I run fast I get out of breath," growled Cheetah.

"The bananas aren't fit to eat," chattered Monkey.

"I'm hunted for my fur," howled Coati.

"The oranges are terrible," bellowed Elephant.

"When I sit on my eggs to hatch them, they break," piped Pelican.

Lion sighed. "My friends, we must do something. Our very lives are in peril. Owl, you are the wise one amongst us. What must we do?"

"During my flights over the forest," said Owl, "I have observed a huge and wondrous object being built. Whoever is building this must be very clever. He should be able to tell us what to do. We must go there at once. Follow me."

They arrived at a huge fence surrounding a strange object. Elephant lifted Lion up so that he could see over the top.

"Extraordinary!" said Lion. "I have never seen anything like it. Whoever is building this must be very clever indeed. We must go in and see him."

They banged on the door. It opened silently, and in they trooped. A man came forward to greet them. "Hello," he said. "My name is Professor Noah. Can I help you?" So Lion explained the problem to him.

"My friends", said Professor Noah, "it is because of what you tell me that I am building this spaceship. It can fly like a bird, but it will go much faster and very much higher. It is going to fly to another planet, another world where the forests will be as beautiful as our forest once was before it was spoiled by pollution. Would you like to come with me?"

"Oh, yes," they all said. "How exciting it will be."

"The spaceship will soon be finished," said Professor Noah. "My robots do most of the work, but I could do with a little help."

And so the animals helped as much as they could. When the spaceship was nearly finished, they all had a very good time playing with the robots.

One day Owl came flying in from one of his trips round the forest and cried in fear, "The forest is on fire. They are not only polluting it – now they are burning it."

"Hurry," cried Professor Noah. "We must finish the work quickly." When all was ready, they boarded the spaceship ready for blast-off.

The great spaceship launched into the heavenly skies with a mighty roar, just before the flames reached it. Up and up, faster and faster they soared into space. Suddenly, the great spaceship waggled from side to side.

"Oh dear," said Professor Noah. "One of our time guidance fins has been damaged on take-off. Soon we must travel through a time-zone that will take us hundreds of years into the future and help us reach our new planet. Our time-zone guidance fin must be in the correct position. I need a strong volunteer to go into space and twist the fin back into shape."

"I'll go," said Elephant. He put on a special space-suit, went out through the air-lock, and pulled the fin into shape. Professor Noah gave him ten oranges and called him a hero.

For forty days and forty nights they travelled through space. The further they went the sadder the animals became. They were very homesick.

At last they approached their new planet. Professor Noah asked the dove to bring back a leaf from a tree to make sure that all was well there. He then tested it in his computer. "Why, I can't believe it," he cried. "This is a leaf from planet Earth. I must check my calculations."

After making many checks, he called a meeting. "My friends", he said, "when Elephant went out to repair our time guidance system, he must have twisted it the wrong way. We have travelled backwards in time, back to planet Earth as it was many hundreds of years ago, before it was polluted."

"Does that mean that we have come back to Earth as it was in the beginning?" asked Lion.

"Yes," said Professor Noah. "It is a wonderful world and we must keep it that way."

As the sun rose, the spaceship descended to Earth. The animals all thanked Professor Noah for saving them. And then they left joyfully for their new homes. "How lovely it is!" they all cried.

"Yes," said Otter, "and thank goodness for all the rain. There seems to have been some flooding here."

Adapted by Jean Gilbert
from 'Professor Noah's Spaceship' by Brian Wildsmith

General notes

The two world problems of pollution and conservation are raised in this story, which could refer to any country. The songs and suggested activities are more suitable for older children.

1 Ask questions about the story.
How did pollution affect the forest animals? What did they decide to do? Why did Professor Noah build the spaceship? What caused the spaceship to travel backwards instead of forwards in time? How might the story have ended if the spaceship had travelled forwards in time to a new planet?

2 Encourage the children to retell the story and to write and illustrate their stories with, perhaps, a different ending.

3 Build up a frieze from the children's paintings and collage cutouts. One idea might be to have a large model of the spaceship in the centre with the polluted and burnt forest on one side and a natural, healthy forested area on the other.

4 The story could lead to a general study of wildlife at risk. Individual children or small groups could study specific animals. The following table lists some examples.

Giant panda (China)	At risk because of dwindling supplies of its food plant, bamboo
Mountain gorilla (Zaire, Rwanda, Uganda)	Suffering from deforestation and hunters
Indian rhinoceros (India, Nepal)	Destruction of habitat and hunted for its horn
Blue whale (many seas)	Hunted for food and for its oil
Cheetah (Africa, Asia)	Destruction of habitat and hunted for its fur
Otter (UK)	Destruction and pollution of its habitat (hunting now illegal)

Stock up the classroom library with suitable information and picture books.

5 The children could also be encouraged to become more aware of their own environment. They could look at local bird life, butterflies and wild flowers in neighbouring parks and open spaces. This would lead naturally to a consideration of how they themselves could help to protect the environment.

Useful addresses

The Council for Environmental Education, School of Education, University of Reading, London Road, Reading RG1 5AQ. Send sae plus 30p for resource sheet on 'The Natural Environment' (primary). Also available: free leaflets about wildlife and plants. Send sae.

Friends of the Earth, 377 City Road, London EC1V 1NA.

Junior Education Special No. 25 is on wildlife conservation and focuses on British species. Copies £1.25 (incl. p & p) from Scholastic Publications Ltd, Westfield Road, Southam, nr Leamington Spa, Warwickshire CV33 OJH.

Learning through Action, Cumberland Road, Reading, Berks RG1 5SR. Educational theatre group visits schools, working closely with children and teachers. Programmes include 'Waste Not Want Not', suitable for 5 to 7 age range.

Nature Conservancy Council, Northminster House, Peterborough PE1 1UA (also has regional offices).

World Wide Fund For Nature, Panda House, Weyside Park, Catteshall Lane, Godalming, Surrey GU7 1XR. Publishes wallcharts and other relevant literature. Send A4 sae plus first-class stamp for full catalogues.

Movement

Introduction to the animals

Ask the children to describe each animal, its size, the way it moves, its habitat, what it eats and how it gets its food. Collect as many pictures as possible. Link up the work with relevant poems. Refer to the descriptions below. This can initially be done with or without accompaniment as desired.

Lion

Large tambour Children imagine a large, powerful cat. Supple, controlled bodies; stealthy, feline movements when prowling; big leaps, occasional pounces; preening and washing after a meal; gentle and drowsy at rest; a few roars.

Cheetah

Small tambour Again, cat-like movements, but smaller in comparison with lion. The fastest of all short-distance runners. Children practise taking off at speed with great control, occasionally slowing down to move through undergrowth, then off again.

Monkey

Tambourine Strong arms, bent legs. Children occasionally move on all fours. They imitate tree-climbing, looking for fruit, peeling bananas, gathering in families. Occasional 'chattering'.

Coati

Wood block Small, furry, cat-sized creature, racoon family, long pointed snout used for digging, large tail for balancing in trees. Walks slowly on flat feet but is a good climber. Sleeps in trees, semi-nocturnal, eats anything. Children improvise sequence on ground and in trees.

Elephant

Alto xylophone or *bass drum* Large and majestic, plodding movements, turning, waving and curling trunk, stretching high for leaves on trees. Children change speed from a plod to an amble to a rush. A few trumpetings.

Pelican

Alto glockenspiel Big, ungainly, rather comic-looking bird with distinct waddle on land. Children puff out bodies and waddle with slightly bent knees, heads appearing to cope with very large beak. Flight is measured and powerful. Children's arms beat slowly with broad controlled movements. To catch fish, birds congregate in crescent shape, drive shoals into shallower water for a catch, then finish their meal on land, doze, digest and fly off again.

Owl

Xylophone   Another large bird. Children make owl shapes as if perched on a tree, shoulders hunched, eyes blinking, head turning from side to side watching for the next meal. Taking off with large arm movements, children circle then swoop down. Back to a tree to eat and watch. Occasional hoots.

The suggested animal sounds may be made, but in a controlled way.

In the forest

Children divide into animal groups and work out between them movement sequences. They give an impression of forest life, moving and stopping in a pre-arranged grouping or order, or responding to instrumental accompaniment. They may wish to exclude some of the animals in the story and/or include some of their own.

Professor Noah and the spaceship

Children decide what kind of man Noah might have been – young, old, tall, short, fat, thin, bespectacled, bearded. . .? They each interpret a Noah working on the spaceship, drawing up plans, programming his robots through a large computer, supervising everything.

Children discuss the robots. Are they imaginary ones that look like mechanized humans, or are they robotic arms like the ones used in factories? (See also pages 110–11.)

An amusing movement sequence can be built around the idea of the animals helping Noah, then playing with the robots. Children decide in what way each animal can help. The elephant could do all the heavy work, moving, lifting, pushing; the monkey could help – or hinder – the computing; the owl and pelican could use their beaks for making holes, tapping in nails . . .

Musical activities

Much of the children's music-making can support the movement, extending the suggestions given in the last section. Here are some general suggestions:

Sound-maker	Ideas for the music
Lion Tambour with padded beater	Prowling – slow beat Running – quicker beat Leaping – short sharp beats, stop Eating/resting – scratch tambour head
Cheetah Small tambour	As for lion
Monkey Tambourine	Tree climbing – shake and strike Playing – scratch and shake
Guiro	Eating, chattering
Coati Wood block	Walking – play slowly Climbing – play quickly Digging – scrape across the top
Elephant Alto xylophone	Plodding, ambling – two low notes played slowly Gathering, eating leaves – shake beater over several high notes
Bass drum	Rushing, charging – a rumble
Pelican Alto glockenspiel	Waddling – a series of two adjacent notes struck together gives a comical effect Flying – glides up and down
Owl Xylophone	Flying – glides up and down Watching – random notes Hoots – vocal sounds

Professor Noah's Spaceship

Small groups of children could work together to compose a short piece of music for each animal. Several groups could then combine to create a musical impression of animals in the forest. Here are some simple suggestions:

The forest background

Leaves rustling	Shakers	
Insects/snakes	Sand blocks	Small group of children work out a sequence
Birds	Recorders trilled occasionally	

Here are just two possible arrangements:

1 Several groups of children play their animal music in a pre-arranged order against a continuous background of forest sounds.

2 This is a more dramatic, story-based sound picture. The forest background sounds continuously. A group of monkeys play around, then rush up a tree to pick bananas and chatter. They quieten as a lion and a cheetah prowl through the undergrowth and disappear. A pelican flies overhead. The monkeys finish their bananas and play in the trees. Soon they are tired. An owl hoots. All the sounds fade.

Making up tunes

See Introduction, page 10. Read the following poem to the children. They could make up a simple tune for the chorus and add accompanying sound(s) to the spoken verses.

We're using up the world

CHORUS We're using up the world,
　　　　　Can't you see?
　　　　　Saying that it's all
　　　　　For you and me.
　　　　　We're using up the world,
　　　　　One more time,
　　　　　And taking away
　　　　　What's yours and mine.

1 I've seen the mighty redwoods　　　*Slow beat on tambour*
Standing a hundred feet high,
Then along came the loggingmen
And chopped them all down　　　　　*Wood block*
And left a big hole in the sky.　　　　*Cymbal*

2 Factories by the thousand　　　　　*Guiro*
Are turning the rivers black,
And the working man says:
"It's hard to make a living　　　　　*Individual, or small group*
But easy to turn your back."　　　　　*(spoken)*

3 Smoke and dust and oil and soot   *Shakers/sand block*
   Fill every breath we breathe,
   So now it costs us our very life
   To have what once was free.   *Triangle*

4 We can always blame the government
   Or men in foreign lands,
   But we're the ones   *Tambourine struck, then shaken*
   Who've covered the green
   With rusty old cars and tin cans.

5 We can always sing this song again,
   Or tell a story told before,
   But we cannot make earthy things   *Tambour, beaten*
   Live and breathe once more.   *Triangle on 'live', 'breathe'*

Suzanne Harris

We're us-ing up the world,— Can't you see?—— Say-ing that it's all—— For you and me.—— We're us|-ing up the world,—— One more time,—— And tak-ing a-way—— what's yours and mine.——

The chorus

Use the pentatonic group of notes on G: G A B D E G. This can produce a tune suitable for the range of the descant recorder. The example here uses notes in the order D E G A B.

Music for listening and moving

Carnival of the Animals Saint-Saëns: 'Lion', 'Elephant' and other suitable extracts.

Noye's Fludde Britten: Short excerpts – animals entering the Ark, 'Kyrie-eleison', the dove, animals leaving the Ark.

Listen, Move and Dance: 'Journey to the Moon' (MV CLP 3531).

Out of this world: Sound Effects (MRMC): Section on 'Outer Space' has rocket take-off, galactic travel, spaceship control room.

BBC Sound Effects No. 6: Section on 'The Zoo' has sounds for parrots, elephants roaring and trumpeting, lions, chimpanzees, tawny owls.

Africa

Words and music by pupils of The Butts County Primary School Hampshire
Arrangement by Christopher Norton

Professor Noah's Spaceship

Man comes a-long and | us-es his gun, | Makes lots of mo-ney or | just has fun.._

Af - ri - ca.

2 There's the desert, the swamp and the ocean deep,
   There's the river and the jungle that we want to keep.
   Man comes along and clears the way,
   Takes all our food and homes away.

   CHORUS Africa! Africa! etc.

3 There are societies, researchers and scientists,
   There are organizations, conservationists.
   They come along and shout "Hey, wait!
   Stop what you're doing before it's too late!"

   CHORUS Africa! Africa! etc.

Suggested percussion

Verse 1

WOOD BLOCK (first three lines)

Verse 2

MARACAS (first three lines)

Verse 3

WOOD BLOCK and MARACAS as above

Leave them a flower

Words and music by Wally Whyton

With movement

VERSE

1 I speak on be - half of the next gen - er - a - tion, My
2 You plun - der, you pil - lage, you tear and you tu - nnel, (𝄽)

sons and my daugh - ters, their chil - dren to come.
Trees ly - ing top - pled, roots fin - ger the sky.

What will you leave them for their re - cre - a - tion? An
Buil - ding a land for ma - chines and com - pu - ters. In the

oil slick, a py - lon, an in - dus - tri - al slum?
name of pro - gress the farms have to die.

3 When the last flower has dropped its last petal,
When the last concrete is finally laid,
The moon will shine cold on a nightmarish landscape,
Your gift to our children, the world which you've made.

Note An extra verse to this song is supplied on the cassette tape

Eggo the Robot

Eggo was a robot. He had one strong arm and he worked on Mr Jones' egg farm packing eggs.

Every day he was hard at work in the packing shed. To his left was an enormous wooden crate filled with thousands of eggs. To his right a conveyor belt carried a steady stream of little cardboard egg boxes, each with six empty cups. Eggo's job was to fill the boxes. Minute after minute, hour after hour, he swung his arm to the left, lowered it towards the crate, carefully picked up an egg, swung his arm to the right and gently placed the egg in a box. When this was full, the conveyor belt moved it on and brought along the next box.

He took exactly five seconds to pick up an egg and put it in a box, and he did this without a pause right through the day. "I'm Mr Jones' star worker," he thought. "I've been packing eggs for months and months and never dropped or cracked a single one." But that very morning, he was to have a surprise.

The work was going perfectly. The beautiful green paint on Eggo's jointed arm gleamed in the sunlight. Everything was spotless. That's how Mr Jones liked to keep things. Even Eggo's black base, containing the computer that gave him his instructions, was spotless. His electric motors buzzed contentedly, his well-oiled gear wheels whirred smoothly and the conveyor belt clicked softly as the egg boxes moved along. Outside, chickens clucked; tractors started and stopped; workers called to one another; a lorry drove off laden with eggs for the shops.

At half past twelve Mr Jones rang the farm bell for the lunch break. He glanced into the packing shed to check that all was well and then went out leaving Eggo working. Eggo didn't need to stop for meals as, like all robots, he ate electricity. He enjoyed being left on his own and began to sing his favourite song to the rhythm of his steady movements:

"Swing to the left, swing to the right,
I can do this day and night,
Pick an egg up and put it down,
I'm the smartest robot in town."

He had just started the second verse when it happened. Eggo lowered the next egg as carefully as ever into the cardboard box. But his arm continued to move down. Squish! The shell cracked and sticky egg mixture squirted out. Each time, he crunched an egg as he put it into the box. Each time, more egg mixture squirted out. A pool of the sticky, slippery yellow mixture began to spread in all directions. Eggo's beautiful green paint was smeared with a mess that oozed into his gear wheels, making them run jerkily and noisily. The rollers of the conveyor grated with annoyance.

Worse was to come. With a sudden screech of gears, Eggo plunged his arm up to the elbow into the wooden crate that had been filled just before lunch. He pumped his arm steadily up and down. A rhythmic, crunching, sloshing sound filled the shed as the eggs were smashed. Egg mixture flew in all directions, drenching Eggo and getting into all his motors and gears.

At last the wooden crate fell apart and egg mixture flooded across the floor. With a final squawk of gears, Eggo juddered and stopped. His forearm dangled uselessly and his once shining hand was now invisible beneath a thick coating of egg.

There was a dreadful silence, disturbed only by occasional glugs and plops. Outside all was calm and peaceful. The workers were in the canteen; Mr Jones was in his office; the engines of the tractors had been switched off; even the hens had stopped clucking.

Then the bell rang for everyone to start work again. Mr Jones took the bunch of keys off the hook in his office and set out to unlock the packing shed. He stopped abruptly as he reached it. A thin but distinct stream of egg was trickling under the door. "Can Eggo have dropped an egg at last?" he wondered. As he opened the door the stream became a river. When he looked in he could hardly believe his eyes. His neat, clean packing shed was now a disgusting yellow mess. In the distance Eggo stood motionless and miserable.

Mr Jones squelched across the floor towards Eggo. "You madman!" he shouted. "You criminal! You. . . you. . ." Words failing him, he stamped his foot with rage. Unfortunately, this caused a jet of cold and slimy egg mixture to spurt up the inside of his trouser leg. Startled, he lost his balance and fell with a loud splosh – flat on his back into the egg.

Mr Jones struggled to his knees, coated with egg and with half an eggshell perched on his head like a tiny hat. He slipped again, landing close to Eggo's base. Then he saw the cause of the trouble. A cable that linked Eggo with the computer was broken. He remembered that one of the workers had accidentally damaged it earlier that morning and he had forgotten to check it before lunch. It must have snapped during the lunch hour, so Eggo was not to blame after all. He patted Eggo with a slimy hand. "Sorry I shouted at you, old chap," he said. "My fault entirely. We will soon have you right again."

Mr Jones cautiously waded back to the door to phone for the robot engineer and to get some of the workers to clean up the shed. Then he went home to clean himself up. His wife could hardly keep a straight face when she saw him. However, she could not resist saying, "If I wring you out, I will get enough egg to make a dozen cakes which everyone can share." Mr Jones, being a good cook as well as a kindly man, helped her. The cakes tasted quite nice, all things considered.

The engineer took Eggo to pieces, removed all traces of egg, fitted a new specially strong cable, and soon had him back in full working order. When the engineer had gone, Mr Jones offered Eggo a slice of cake to make up for shouting at him. Eggo nodded and buzzed politely, but secretly he preferred electricity.

Based on an idea by Leslie Gilbert

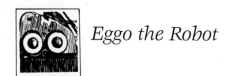 *Eggo the Robot*

General notes

Computers are rapidly becoming an essential part of the mechanics of everyday life, making their way into factories, offices, homes and schools. This story is about one of the ways in which they can be used to control robots, and features the kind of robot with a mechanical 'arm' that is used in industry today.

The following suggestions outline classroom activities that can extend the story with older children.

1 Ask the children questions about the story. Ask them about the farm where Eggo worked. What kind of man was Mr Jones and how did he run his farm? Describe some of the other kinds of work that might have gone on there. Why did Eggo go wrong and when did this happen? How did the engineer get Eggo to work properly again?

2 Encourage the children to describe in detail the various episodes of the story.

3 The children could write and illustrate the story or one episode in detail. Assemble their work in a class story book.

4 Build up a class information library.

5 Ask the children to collect pictures of robots from illustrated magazines and to find out about ways in which robots are used. This will entail some research outside school, at home, in the local library, around local factories and offices, etc.

6 The children's craft work in junk modelling and model-making will reflect this research.

7 Develop the principle of the computer–robot relationship. The children work with partners, one as the computer giving instructions, the other responding as the robot. The task is to put an egg (ping-pong ball) into an empty egg box. As with Eggo, the egg could be on the left of the robot and the egg box on the right. Each time the instruction is carried out, the robot signals back 'Done' or something similar.

Computer	Robot
Move your arm 20 cm to the left.	Done
Move your arm 10 cm down.	Done
Fingers down.	Done
Grip egg.	Done
And so on.	

The children could go on to work out a full set of operational instructions in words for other types of jobs and try them out on a friendly 'robot'.

Movement

A general introduction to mechanical movement can lead into more specific robotic movement.

1 Moving around
Children move in stiff-jointed fashion forwards/backwards, left/right, stopping/starting. They can incorporate head and arm movements, then go on to work out a short sequence that can be repeated several times. This is best done unaccompanied as each child will have a different rhythm, speed and set of movements.

2 Introduce sound codes. The children respond as computerized robots, for example:

Wood block	Move forward
Drum	Move back
Guiro	Move up and down on the spot
Triangle struck	Turn right (90 degrees)
Triangle trilled	Turn left (90 degrees)

It may be necessary to divide the class for this. Choose children from one group to make the sounds while the other group responds.

3 Play a game with a volunteer who agrees to be blindfolded. Sit the rest of the children in a circle and choose a sound group. Their job will be to move the 'robot' from one point A to another point, B. Starting at A, turn the robot round several times. The sound codes will be made according to the robot's position in relation to B.

4 Moving parts of the body
Relate this activity to machines in general. Children can get ideas from working machines like a car engine, an egg whisk, a lawn-mower. Try out different machine-like movements using the whole body first, then later different parts of the body. Movements can go up and down, to and fro, in and out, round and round. They can go quickly or slowly, straight or zigzag, or be twisted. They can be smooth or they can shake or vibrate. No accompaniment is needed at this stage.

5 Ask the children to work out a short sequence that can be repeated several times and to add their own vocal sounds. Divide the class into groups so that ideas can be shared. Children can choose to work with one or two others.

6 Introduce instrumental sound as a stimulus. Discuss with the children what sounds would be suitable for the different kinds of movement. Cymbals might accompany long sustained movements, wood blocks short quick movements, shakers twisty and shaking movements. They could be used in a number of ways, for example:

Mirror movement Children work with a partner. Concentrate on smooth, sustained movement. Cymbal or chime bar plays and the first child responds with a movement. The sound is repeated and the second child mirrors the movement. Continue, letting the children change over. Repeat with a different instrument.

Groups Children work with a partner, one moving, the other playing. They team up with another pair to work out an interesting pattern of movement and sound.

The big machine Keeping to the same partner idea, divide the class. Half the children – the players – sit in a large circle, with the other half – the movers – in the middle. To begin with, all movers sit in the circle in front of their partner.

The machine begins with one child moving in the middle. The others join in one by one in pre-arranged order to form a kaleidoscopic picture in movement and sound. Let the children decide how to end. The machine could slow down and eventually stop. It could be 'turned off', and everyone could freeze at a signal, or the children in the centre could return to their places in reverse order, to represent a dismantling of the machine.

7 Robot ballet
This idea could be related to a project on cars. The robots have jointed 'elbows' and 'wrists' and several 'fingers'. The range of movement is very similar to that of the human arm.

Work on cars done by robots includes welding, spraying and paint checking. Four robots work on one car at a time, each robot stationed at one corner and programmed to work on a specific area of the frame.

The ballet could comprise groups of four children as robots stationed around imaginary cars. Each group is engaged on a different job. They continually stop and start as they finish a car and the next one is brought along.

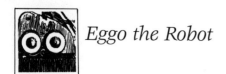 *Eggo the Robot*

Musical activities

Machine sounds

Discuss with the children the kinds of sounds that different machines make in relation to the movement they produce. If possible, bring in some domestic machines like an egg whisk, a small typewriter, a food processor, and get the children to listen to them carefully. Try to make a recording inside a local car repair shop or of some roadworks.

Encourage the children to find words to describe the sounds and to improvise vocal, body and instrumental sounds to go with them, for example:

	Vocal/body	Instrumental
Buzz	z z z z z z	Sand block/shaker
Click	t t t t t t	Sticks/tapped triangle
Whirr	r r r r r r	Tambour/drum head scratched

Sequences can now be improvised. Sounds can be loud or quiet, quick or slow. They can get louder/quieter, quicker/slower and can include rhythmic repeating patterns, for example:

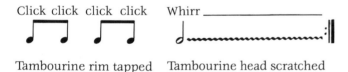

Tambourine rim tapped   Tambourine head scratched

Sound pictures

Improvise some sound pictures according to the children's previous experience (see 'Introduction', pages 8–9). Here are some suggestions for approaches at different levels:

1   Using voices only, children make machine sounds at random, or in pre-arranged order or groups. They will decide on speed and dynamics.

2   Use instruments in a similar way.

3   The musical machine
This could be a purely imaginative composition based on machine-like sounds and on specific musical rhythms. Some aspect of musical form could be introduced as outlined in the 'Introduction', page 9. For example:

Group A

WOODEN INSTRUMENTS

sticks   guiro

Group B

METAL INSTRUMENTS

triangle   finger   cymbals

Group C

DRUMS/TAMBOURS

scratched   tapped

Group D

TUNED INSTRUMENTS

low, high, low, high   slide   slide

Suggested arrangement: A B A C A D A, with each group repeating their sequence an agreed number of times.

Dramatizing the story

Ask the children to make up a tune for Eggo's song (see Introduction, page 10).

Work out with the children sound sequences that could support a dramatized version of the story. The descriptive words of the story will guide the children's choice of instruments and sound effects.

Story line	Suggested sounds
Eggo works in the packing shed	
Electric motors buzzing	Voices
Gear wheels whirring smoothly	Shakers
Conveyor belt clicking quietly	Sticks
Farm sounds	
Chickens clucking	Voices
Tractors starting/stopping	Guiro and sand block
Workers calling	Voices
Lunch hour	Whistle
(*Farm sounds stop*)	
Eggo's song	Voices
Eggo goes wrong	
Eggs cracking	Crackle glossy paper, for example from inside a chocolate box
Egg mixture squirting out	Bowl of water and cloth
Gear wheels screeching	Guiro
Wooden crate falls apart	Sticks and drum
Mr Jones inspects	
End of lunch hour	Whistle
Squelches and plops	Water and cloth
Engineer comes	
Mends cable and cleans Eggo	Sand block and sticks
Eggo starts work again	*As beginning*

(See also song 'Go, go, robot' on pages 114–16.)

Music for listening and moving

'In the Hall of the Mountain King' from *Peer Gynt* Suite   Grieg

Listen, Move and Dance No. 4, Side 2: 'Machines' (EMI CLP 3531)

'Machines and Robots' from *Child Education: Music and Movement* cassette (Scholastic Publications Ltd, Westfield Road, Southam, Leamington Spa, Warks. CV33 OJH)

The Sorcerer's Apprentice   Dukas

Much modern and pop music would be suitable. Ask the children to make a selection from their own records and cassettes.

Eggo the Robot

Go, go, robot

Moderate

INTRODUCTION

Chris Adams and Michael Sullivan

VERSE

1 Ro-bot work-ing on a farm _____ With an au-to-ma-ted arm, _____
2 Ro-bots ne-ver need to take _____ Break-fast, tea or din-ner breaks, _____

His com-pu-ter, you can tell, _____ Con-trols him ve-ry well. _____
Plain e-lec-tric food is best _____ For ro-bots to di-gest. _____

CHORUS

Left, left, robot -right, right, ro-bot, Not too fast,

not too slow-bot, Not too high, not too low-bot,
(**V. 3** LOTS too low-bot,)

Go, go, robot _ go, go, robot, Go, go, robot _ GO! ____
(**V. 3** Oh no, robot _ oh no, robot, Oh no, robot _ OH!) ___

Eggo the Robot

3 Robots never make a mess,
But one Tuesday, can you guess?
Programmed into Eggo's song
Is how the job went wrong.

CHORUS
Left, left, robot, right, right, robot,
(*2 bars of sound effects: chocolate-box cracklings*)

Not too fast, not too slow-bot,
Not too high, LOTS too low-bot,

(*4 bars of sound effects: cymbal followed either by
more cracklings and squelches from children or
plunger in bowl of water according to children's
ideas.*)

Oh no, robot – oh no, robot,
Oh no, robot – OH!

(*More sound effects, then final crash from sticks
and drum as wooden crate falls apart.*)

4 Eggo's mended, you can see,
Now he's working perfectly,
Picking, packing, problems gone,
No need to egg him on!

Final CHORUS   Left, left, robot, etc.

Percussion

INTRODUCTION   VERSE

CHORUS

Margaret and the Mermaid

There was once a young woman called Margaret who was so beautiful that her fame spread to every corner of the island of Tobago and many songs were composed about her. Margaret was also an excellent swimmer, equally at home in river and sea.

She was swimming in the sea one day when a man suddenly appeared beside her. He was young and handsome and soon they were chatting like two old friends. After a while the man said to Margaret, "There are some lovely underwater gardens not far from here, but you would have to be a strong swimmer to get there. Are you a good swimmer, Margaret?"

Margaret was taken aback when he spoke her name for she had not told it to him. However, she replied, "I have been told that I'm like a fish in water."

"You have no fear of the sea then?" he enquired.

"I fear the sea as much as I fear the land. No more, no less," said Margaret.

"Right then, let us see what kind of fish you are," he said. And seizing her hand he dived so swiftly that before she knew it, she was in a large hall with walls of coral, festooned with sea-green vines. The rooms which led off from the hall were a sight to behold and were paved with marble floors that shone like glass.

There Margaret saw her companion fully for the first time and realized that he was no mortal man but a mermaid. She was not afraid of him, for he continued to treat her with the utmost courtesy. She herself had an open curiosity about everything and was fascinated by the spectacular undersea gardens which the mermaid showed her. There was so much to see that Margaret was surprised when he said to her, "You have been with us for three days. Would you like to stay and be my true companion, Margaret?"

"Three days! Why, I thought I had been here only a few hours. How is it that I have neither eaten nor slept and I feel none the worse for it?" asked Margaret.

"Time feels different here because of the flow of water. But tell me Margaret, will you stay?"

Margaret did not know what to do or say. To tell the truth she was in love with this gentle man of the sea who treated her like a princess. But to stay with him meant that she would never see her folk and friends again. She was clever enough not to provoke his anger with a hasty refusal, so she said, "Let me think about it for a little longer."

Now that she knew he wanted her to stay, Margaret was careful about what she consumed. She had once been told that these beings could bewitch people by giving them certain things to eat and drink. So she drank only clear water and ate only sea-grapes. Finally she told the mermaid that she wished to return to her world.

"I am likely to die from homesickness if I stay with you," she said. And since he loved her truly, he let her go and took her up through what seemed to be a special tunnel to the beach nearest her village. But before they parted, he gave her a beautiful stone which reflected the colours of the rainbow when it was held up to the sun.

"It will ensure a long and full life, and good fortune will be with you always," said the mermaid when he gave it to her.

And so it was. She lived to be over a hundred years old and she never lost her beauty. She never moved from her village near the sea and asked to be buried at sea when she died.

Grace Hallworth

General notes

Legends about mermaids are said to have originated from early sightings of sea-cows, manatees and dugongs. These supernatural creatures feature in stories told in many countries, especially those near the sea, and names may vary according to local legend. In this country there are stories about mermaids that are young girls, half fish, half human, but in Tobago, according to local tradition mermaids are male in sex and fairymaids are female. The children will also be interested to learn that usually, mermaids are at work in the sea in the day while fairymaids occupy themselves in the rivers. Both beings are said to be 'fallen spirits', partaking of the nature of gods in the ability to bestow on mortals both good and evil.

The story of Margaret's encounter with a mermaid is simple, yet dramatic. The following suggestions for classroom activities extend the story for older children, but, suitably adapted, can be enjoyed by younger children as well.

1   Ask questions about the story.
In what ways was life under the sea different from that on land for Margaret? Why did Margaret take time to answer the mermaid's invitation to stay with him? What reason did she give for asking to return to her home? Why did the mermaid agree to take her back? How did he show his concern for her?

2   The story could be retold from the point of view of Margaret or even of the mermaid. What might Margaret's thoughts have been on her return home? What might she have told her family? What kind of story might she have told her own children, years later?

3   The story could lead to some imaginative accounts of Margaret's underwater adventure: the sea gardens, the exotic coral landscape of the mermaid's world and the sea creatures living there. Have available some good picture reference books like *The Caribbean and the Gulf of Mexico*, ed. Pat Hargreaves (Wayland, 1980).

4   Build up an underwater frieze to relate to the children's stories and to any movement that is introduced (see 'Movement' notes below).

5   Find out about life in the Caribbean. Some of the children may have relatives living there. They may be able to bring in pictures or ask their parents to come and talk to the class, perhaps to help with cooking some Caribbean food.

Movement

The sea and seafood are very important to life in the Caribbean. Big trawlers work far out at sea and freeze their fish on board. Local fishermen use small boats and canoes with outboard motors, and lines, nets and traps to catch all kinds of tropical fish and shellfish. These are usually sold to fishermen's cooperatives or to local merchants for sale at the markets.

The sea itself is a mixed blessing. It is warm and in calm weather can be an ocean paradise, but in summer and early autumn great storms and hurricanes arise, causing widespread damage.

A general introduction to movement could be based on the various moods of the sea.

Calm sea

Shakers   Start with gentle ripples in the fingers, hands, arms, shoulders. Relaxed bodies, children begin to move gently, then trace rounded shapes.
Glockenspiel   Explore different levels, indicating pools, lagoons, open sea – working in small or large groups.

Seashore

Shakers/glockenspiel   Small waves break and ripple over the sand. Extend arms for the ripples, little runs, then lower arms.

Margaret and the Mermaid

Choppy sea

Tambourine Movements are broader, children travel faster with spins and small leaps.

Big rollers

Broader movements and level changes.

Breakers

Tambourine, rustled/struck Foaming white breakers crash against coral reefs on a windy day. Children curve arms overhead, rush forward, stretch high, then 'crash'.

Hurricane

Warm mist blows from all directions towards the hurricane; blows around the centre or 'eye'; travels and is eventually broken up by mountains or cool land air.
Tambourine, drum Children are spread out. They travel to the centre, then whirl round and travel in a group. Meeting cooler air – a group of children – they part, stop whirling and find a place to sink down.

Sea creatures and seashore life

Water's edge

Green turtle

Egg hatches out in sand, young turtle moves laboriously towards the sea, then swims free.
Shaker Children curl up, slowly emerge from shell, move on tummies propelled by arms and legs.
Glockenspiel Stand up gently to swim away.

Crabs

Crawl, swim, hide among rocks, burrow beneath sand.
Drum head, scratched Children move crab-like, crouched on all fours; they work out sequence of movement.

Wading birds

Wander about probing sand with long bills.
Xylophone Children walk with arms folded back, heads down, searching for food; walk carefully, legs lifted high and placed down carefully. An occasional quick strike to catch food.

Children improvise sequence representing seashore life, some moving, some playing percussion.

Shallow water near coral reef

Sponges

Slides on glockenspiel Children stand or crouch with rounded bodies, expand and contract gently.

Anemones

Slides on glockenspiel Children stand or sit. Bodies move, arms wave gently.

Coral

Children form rocky and spiky shapes.

Small fish

Soprano glockenspiel Darting, hovering movements. Small groups work together.

Lobsters

Guiro Children crawl about, travel suddenly, arms extended.

Sharks and barracuda

Large fish visit reef by day to prey on smaller creatures. Great barracuda have long streamlined bodies; swim very fast; attack ferociously.
Tambour Children's movement can reflect an attack.

Parrot-fish

Tambourine, rustled and scraped   Children swim about scraping coral with 'beaks'.

Children improvise sequence representing underwater coral reef, some moving, some playing percussion.

The open sea

The open sea near the islands is very clear. Large golden clumps of seaweed called sargassum float on the surface, sheltering myriads of tiny shrimps, crabs and baby fish which provide food for larger fish that often swim along with the drifting seaweed.

Jellyfish

Shakers   Children 'float' with limp bodies, arms dangling. The Portuguese man-of-war is a large jellyfish with stinging tentacles. Several children could group together for this.

Flying fish

Glockenspiel   Leap into air to escape larger fish, spreading fins like wings for gliding. Children move swiftly, then spread arms for flight.

Big fish

Include mackerel, marlin, sailfish and sharks.

Deeper waters

Here there is no light from the sun. Many creatures living in the depths have light organs on their bodies rather like tiny lamps.

Squid

Tambourine   Children move about in little spurts, arms waving as tentacles.

Sea floor

Shakers   Starfish, brittlestars, small shrimps and lobsters live here. Children form shapes, moving gently in the mud.

Musical activities

Rockpool	Suggested sounds
Water	Gentle slides up and down xylophone. Random notes on chime bars or several chimes played with thin card or ruler wobbled over sound hole. Group of children work out sequence.
Seaweed	Shakers rolled gently round.
Sand	Long tube shaker tipped up and down.
Crabs	Drum head scratched, occasionally tapped.
Snall fish	Soprano glockenspiel. Slides for swimming, random notes for darting, tremolo for hiding.

Suggested arrangement

These sound pictures should be gentle, full of quiet, interesting sounds. Begin with the rockpool at low tide with very quiet sounds from the water and sand sections. Crabs crawl by and disappear. The pool fills up as the tide comes in. Water music reflects this. Small fish swim around, crabs swim and crawl, seaweed moves in the water. As the tide goes out, the creatures hide in the shallow waters. Sounds fade away except water and sand which play almost inaudibly.

Margaret and the Mermaid

Coral reef	Suggested sounds
Water	As for rockpool but use alto xylophone.
Anemones and sponges	Alto glockenspiel. Gentle slides up and down; a tremolo over two or three notes. Random notes or simple repetitive melody on metallophone Children work out sequence.
Small tropical fish	Quick slides on soprano glockenspiel. Random notes for darting movements.
Lobsters	Guiro – slowish rasp.
Big fish	Bass xylophone: tremolo for hovering, slides for fast swimming. Add a cymbal shimmer and strikes for an attack on small fish.

Suggested arrangement

For the beginning, ask the children to work out a sequence to suggest life on a coral reef, with sounds from all sections except the one for the big fish; for instance, the water section could provide a background for the other sounds which come and go. Sounds for the big fish approaching begin. Lobster and anemone sounds fade as music for an attack is built up. The attack over, peaceful life gradually resumes and the sound picture finishes as it began.

These suggestions could form the basis for sound pictures or for accompanying movement sequences.

Poems

Sea creatures

Gibbering in your fishy language
You gossip about other sea creatures,
And we, humans,
Sit, and watch, and wonder.

How is your world?
Are there towns as on earth?
Are there churches?
Are there schools?

Hiding in creeks and crevices,
You wait patiently in silence,
As we do in battle.
Until the enemy, man, passes.

Kill or be killed.
Your rule, it seems,
You follow
To secure your food.

Retiring to a seasome bed,
As night falls
You sleep an uneasy sleep,
Waking at a whisper.

Beginning a new day,
You rise in the morning
And perform similar rituals
To the day before.

Realize now, everyone,
In fish and man
There is no difference
In their way of life.

Maria Gonzalez

This thoughtful poem, written by a young girl, could stimulate discussion among the children in connection with the theme of the story of Margaret's underwater adventure.

Bottom of the sea

	Suggested sounds
Deep, deep down	*Bass drum or large tambour*
At the bottom of the sea, Fish are scuttling endlessly:	
Grey old plodders,	*Shakers*
Bright young friskers,	*Bells*
Fathers, mothers and kiddies in pairs –	*Shakers/bells*
Deep, deep down	*Drum/tambour*
At the bottom of the sea.	
Deep, deep down	*Drum/tambour*
At the bottom of the sea,	
Pirates' treasure chest has broken free –	*Guiro*
Spilling booty	*Shakers*
Of a thousand years:	
Gold and silver bullion of the buccaneers –	*Glockenspiel*
Deep, deep down	*Drum/tambour*
At the bottom of the sea.	
Deep, deep down	*Drum/tambour*
At the bottom of the sea, Where imagination can roam free –	
Coral gardens swamped in light	*Glockenspiel*
Conveying quite a magnificent sight:	
Starfish, brittlestars, lobsters free –	*Guiro*
Yet, did I see	
A mermaid	*Triangle*
At the bottom of the sea?	

Gloria Cameron

The poem above could be incorporated into a dramatized version of the story to support a movement episode. It lends itself to a sound accompaniment; suggestions are given, but ask the children for their own ideas.

Reference books

The Caribbean ed. W. James (Macdonald Educational, Looking at Lands series, 1984)

The Caribbean and the Gulf of Mexico ed. Pat Hargreaves (Wayland, 1980)

West Indies Zaidee Lindsay (A & C Black, 1979)

West Indies Keith Lye (Franklin Watts, 1983)

Poetry and song books

Brown Gal in de Ring (1974), *Dondy Shandy* and *Beeny Bud* (1975), *Alle, Alle, Alle* (1977), collected and arranged for schools by Olive Lewin (Oxford University Press)

Mango Spice ed. Yvonne Conolly (A & C Black, 1981)

Song of the Surreys Telcine Turner (Macmillan, Caribbean series, 1977)

Topic Anthologies for Young Children (Book 3: Caribbean section) Jean Gilbert (Oxford University Press, 1986)

Music for listening and moving

Caribbean Folk Music (Ethnic Folkways Library FE 4533)

Caribbean Island Music (Nonesuch Records, Explore Series H 72047)

Caribbean Songs and Games for Children (Folkways Records FC 7856)

Folkways Records are not readily available in record shops in this country, but can be obtained through some specialist shops like the Folk Record Department of Collet's International Bookshop, 129/131 Charing Cross Road, London WC2. They might also be obtained through local record libraries and resource centres.

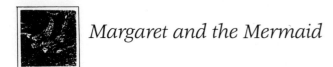

Margaret and the Mermaid

Bottom of the sea

Words by Manley Yong and Gloria Cameron
Music by Chris Cameron

Gently and with movement
Guitar: Capo 1st fret

VERSE

1 Down be - low at the bot-tom of __ the sea, ___
2 Take a trip to the bot-tom of __ the sea, ___

Margaret and the Mermaid

There is one crea - ture_ you rare - ly_ do see._
And feel the cur - rent_ so strong and_ so free._

Beau - ti - ful_ and strong_ with his sun - streaked hair,_
Watch the twist-ing trail_ of the sea - weeds_ go by,_

Could be half fish or half_ hu - man down there._
Dance to the mo - tion of the mov - ing tide._

Margaret and the Mermaid

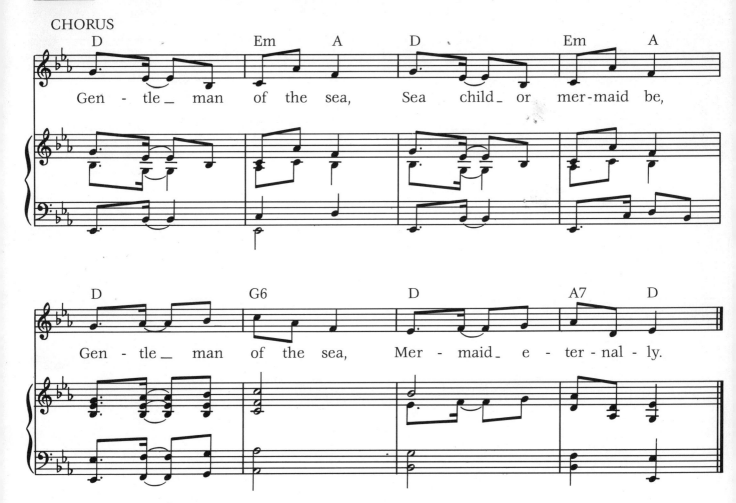

3 Barracuda and silvery cutlass fish,
Swirling and twirling as sharks pass them by,
Multi-coloured creatures a-prancing to and fro,
Whistle a tune, there is no night down there.

CHORUS
Gentle man of the sea,
Sea child or mermaid be,
Gentle man of the sea,
Mermaid eternally.

Sing this beautiful song gently, clearly and
with an easy rhythm. If any percussion is
added, it should be unobtrusive.

The song could be sung as an introduction to
a dramatized version of the story and/or
support an underwater movement episode.